总主编　惠　中

21世纪
小学教师
教育系列教材

小学英语教学设计与案例解析（第二版）

●主编　王融　董玲

中国人民大学出版社
·北京·

作者简介

王融，上海师范大学教育学院副教授，主要从事小学英语教师教育的教学与研究工作。曾主编《教师英语口语训练》《小学英语学科知识与拓展》《小学英语教学设计与案例解析》等著作。

董玲，上海师范大学教育学院初等教育系副教授，小学教育专业硕士生导师，主要从事小学英语教师教育研究，先后开设了“小学英语案例研究”、“中外儿童文学比较”、“英汉翻译技巧”、“学科教育学”（英语）、“专业英语”（研究生）等课程。曾出版《小学英语课程与教学论》等著作。

内容简介

该书主要根据《义务教育英语课程标准（2022年版）》进行修订，以更适合教师教学的需要。本书旨在帮助学生提高英语教学实践能力，主要内容有教学设计的概述，教案设计，小学英语课堂教学准备、呈现、操练、应用、结课等环节的设计和典型案例解析。本书有两大特色：一是案例依照《义务教育英语课程标准（2022年版）》设定的知识和技能的要求，涵盖各种版本教材中语音、词汇、语法、功能、话题等主要内容，实用性强；二是书中教学设计既符合儿童的心理与不同阶段儿童的思维特点，又符合学科英语特点，适合教师教学。本书不仅可以作为小学教育专业的教材，亦可用于在职小学教师的培训，对准备参加教师资格证考试的人也极具参考价值。

总　序

教师是教育事业发展的基础，是提高教育质量、办好人民满意教育的关键。《国务院关于加强教师队伍建设的意见》明确提出，我国教师队伍建设的总体目标是：形成一支师德高尚、业务精湛、结构合理、充满活力的高素质专业化教师队伍。为了实现这一目标，国家加大了教师教育改革的推进力度。2011 年 10 月，教育部颁布了《关于大力推进教师教育课程改革的意见》和《教师教育课程标准（试行）》，对深入推进教师教育课程改革作出了总体部署。2012 年 2 月，教育部正式颁布《幼儿园教师专业标准（试行）》《小学教师专业标准（试行）》《中学教师专业标准（试行）》，将其作为教师培养、准入、培训、考核等工作的重要依据。与此同时，为了严把教师入口关，教育部制定了教师资格考试指导意见和考试标准，对国家教师资格考试制度进行改革。

2018 年初，教育部又制定并颁发《师范类专业认证标准》，借鉴国际高等教育通用的专业认证方式，推进师范类专业建设与课程改革，以保证并提高我国教师教育培养质量。

教育部关于教师教育改革的一系列重大部署对我国教师教育发展将产生积极、深远的影响。其中，“教师专业标准（试行）”明确提出了对合格中小幼教师的专业要求，为促进中小幼教师的专业化发展、建设高素质的教师队伍提供了基本准则；《教师教育课程标准（试行）》则聚焦教师教育课程的改革，其所倡导的基本理念、基本标准和课程模块等，对中小幼教师教育的课程设置、教学内容和培养方式的改革提出了具体、明确的要求；教师资格考试制度改革实行国家统一的教师资格考试，包括笔试和面试，考试成绩合格者方能认定教师资格，这必然对中小幼教师培养产生较大的冲击；师范类专业认证的全面推进，则力图重塑高校师范类专业人才培养体系，建立贯穿教师培养全过程的质量保障机制……这一切，都要求教师教育机构、教师教育工作者和研究者关注教师教育改革的动态，研究和领会教师教育改革的精神，进一步推进教师教育的课程教学改革工作。

在我国近 1 800 万各级各类教师中，小学教师是人数最多、占比最高的一支队伍，小学教师队伍建设是我国教师教育发展的一个重要方面。20 世纪 90 年代以来，随着经济、社会和教育事业的发展，我国三级师范教育体系逐步向二级甚至一级师范教育体系过渡，小学教师培养也经历了由以中专学历为主体，到大学专科和本科学历占主导地位的迅速转型。据不完全统计，目前各类教师教育机构开设的本科小学教育专业有 200 多个，专科初等教育专业也有相当大的规模，形成了庞大的小学教师培养体系。小学教育专业是我国高等师范教育体系中一个全新的专业，经过多年的实践探索和理论研究，专业建设已取得许多重要成果。但毋庸讳言，其专业建设中依然存在着诸如培养模式不够清晰、课程设置不尽合理、课程内容简单照搬、培养方式变化不大等问题。而且，高等教育大众化带来的高等院校升格和结构调整，灵活、开放的教师教育体系构建带来的师范院校的重新定位和内部重组，小学教师培养迅速高学历化带来的培养模式变革，特别是2022年4月教育部颁发的《义务教育课程方案和课程标准（2022年版）》对深入推进义务教育阶段的课程改革进行了全面部署，这些都迫切要求我们回应基础教育课程教学改革的要求，不断创新教师教育课程理念，优化教师教育课程结构，改革课程教学内容，改进教学方法和手段，强化教育实践环节，提高小学教师的培养质量。

加强教学基本建设是专业建设的中心问题之一。课程是组织教学的基本单位，教材则是课程的载体，教材建设涉及教育理念的更新、教学内容的选择和教学方式的变革，加强小学教育专业的教材建设是保证小学教师培养质量的重要方面。高学历小学教师的培养模式、课程体系仍处于探索之中，《教师教育课程标准（试行）》的颁发必然导致小学教师培养课程的结构调整，加之国家教师资格考试制度改革和师范类专业认证的持续推进，新课标提出的小学阶段课程教学改革新举措，对小学教师培养提出了新的要求，这些都应该体现在小学教育专业的教材之中。有鉴于此，我们组织编写了这套“21世纪小学教师教育系列教材”。

在这套教材的组织编写过程中，我们始终坚持并力图实现以下目标：

第一，根据《教育部关于大力推进教师教育课程改革的意见》《教师教育课程标准（试行）》的精神，按照小学教育专业培养模式改革和课程结构调整的要求，精心设计系列教材结构和具体编写项目。我们将本套教材设计为小学教师教育理论系列、小学教师学科教育系列和小学教师教育教学实践系列三个部分，分别针对小学教育专业师范生的教师教育理论课程的学习、主要任教学科专业基础课程的学习和小学教育教学实践能力提升三个方面。在具体教材项目选择方面，则注意与小学教育专业的课程改革和小学阶段的课程方案调整相吻合，除了基本覆盖该专业传统基础课程之外，还设计了《小学教育基础》《小学生认知与学习》《小学数学思维方法》《儿童文学应用教程》《小学语文教学设计与案例分析》《小学数学教学设计与案例分析》《小学班队活动设计》《小学科学活动设计与指导》《小学综合实践活动设计与组织》《小学生心理健康与辅导》等教材，希望能够填补小学教育专业教材建设的一些空白。

第二，根据《小学教师专业标准（试行）》对小学教师的具体要求，参照《义务教育课程方案和课程标准（2022年版）》的基本精神，坚持育人为本的基本理念，全面落实习近平总书记提出的培养有理想、有本领、有担当时代新人的要求，基于小学生核心素养发展的需要，凸显中华优秀传统文化、革命传统、国家安全、生命安全与健康等重大教育主题，精心选择教材编写内容。教育生理和心理都处于迅速成长期的6～12岁儿童，要求小学教师具有良好的师德，要关爱小学生，尊重小学生人格，富有爱心、责任心、耐心和细心等，也要求小学教师具有综合的专业素养，具备合理的知识结构和多方面的专业能力。

我们必须改变长期以来以学科知识体系为主线的教材内容组织方式，按照学生学习逻辑组织呈现课程内容，以小学教师的职业需要为前提，关注小学教育专业师范生培养实际，关注未来小学教师专业素养的养成，关注目前小学新课程改革和国家统编本教材的发展方向，加强与学生经验、现实生活、社会实践的联系，兼顾在职小学教师专业发展和培训的需要，选择合适的教学内容，形成具有自身特色的教材知识体系。

第三，根据国家教师资格考试制度改革的要求，突出实践取向和能力培养，将学科知识、教育理论与教育实践有机结合，以培养未来小学教师教书育人的实践能力。本套教材的编写十分注重从解决小学教育教学实践中的问题出发，其中教育理论知识学习以学生能理解和运用为目的，教育教学实践能力培养注重学生实践体验和反思的过程，同时兼顾国家教师资格考试相关内容与技能训练，以推动小学教师教育的教学方式和学习方式的变革。

第四，在教材的编写体例和内容呈现方式上，本套教材注意学习借鉴国内外相关高等教育教材的成功经验，根据不同的教材系列设计出更加灵活的编写体例，增加更多课堂和教育案例与相关知识专栏。写作语言风格活泼，避免简单的理论说教，以适合当代教育工作者阅读和学习的需要。

组织编写“21世纪小学教师教育系列教材”是一项庞大的系统工程，此项工作得到了全国许多从事小学教师教育的兄弟院校领导的大力支持、中国人民大学出版社领导的直接关心和策划编辑的精心策划，更有赖于各分册主编和编写者的辛勤劳动，对此我们一并表示衷心感谢！

本人从事小学教师教育研究已有20年之久，也先后主持和参与了一些小学教师教育教材建设项目，在自己学术研究和职业生涯的最后阶段，我愿将多年从事小学教师教育研究的成果和经验，将自己参与教育部许多教师教育重大改革项目的思考和启示，运用于本套教材的编写过程中。希望通过各方的积极参与和共同努力，能够编写出反映教师教育改革与发展趋势的、具有特色的小学教师教育教材，为小学教育专业建设和小学教师专业发展尽绵薄之力。

是为序。

惠 中

2022年12月8日于上海

目　录

第一章

教学设计概述

本章导读

我们学习了许多教育教学理论知识，但缺乏教学实践。我们虽然知道教学设计的定义、重要性，但具体该做什么、如何做，心中没有底。第一章就要解决这些问题。在进行小学英语教学设计之前，我们首先要了解小学英语学科的特点，解读英语课程标准的要求，熟悉选用教材的内容。

第一节　小学英语学科的特点

近年来，英语教学得到了社会、学校、家庭的极大关注，社会办学机构开办的英语学习班比比皆是。然而，学校课堂教学仍是小学生学习英语最主要的途径，也是最基本的教学组织形式。英语课作为一种相对固定的教学安排，为学生提供了一种特定的学习条件。教师通过精心设计的课堂教学活动，为学生掌握英语基础知识和提高听、说、读、写能力创造了有利的条件。学生通过参与课堂教学活动，逐步获得综合语言运用能力。教师了解小学英语学科的特点，了解教学对象，也就是了解小学生的年龄特征与心理特点，对教学设计和教学实施都至关重要。

学生心理发展的阶段是以年龄为标志的。不同年龄阶段的学生有不同的心理特征。这种年龄特征是指儿童的年龄阶段特征，而不是指某一个年龄的某一个特征。我国儿童心理学家根据儿童心理学的研究成果和长期的教育实践经验，把人从出生到成熟的心理发展过程划为六个时期：乳儿期、婴儿期、幼儿期、童年期、少年期和青年初期。小学阶段相当于其中的童年期。童年期儿童的感知特点、注意特点、记忆特点和思维特点在教育心理学书籍中都有论述，这里就不重复了。教师只有了解掌握了低年级、中年级、高年级小学生的年龄特征和心理特点，才能遵循小学生认识事物的规律来设计和实施英语课堂教学。心理学研究证明，学生学习时参与的感觉器官越多，理解和掌握知识的效果越好。英语教学要尽可能调动学生的视觉、听觉和触觉，使其眼、耳、口、手、脑多通道协作来进行听、说、读、写的全面训练。小学生有意注意的时间跨度短，教师在教学中要善于交替使用有意注意和无意注意，运用丰富的教学活动，动静结合，合理安排语言的输入与输出，既要考虑学生注意的情绪因素，也要重视锻炼学生控制自己情绪的能力。教师在教学活动中要遵循儿童的记忆规律，利用无意识记忆，提高有意识记忆，采用不同的记忆方法提高学生的记忆效果。在整个小学阶段，学生的思维特点是从以形象思维为主逐步过渡到以抽象思维为主，教学活动的设计也要符合学生在低、中、高三个阶段不同的思维特点。低年级的教学生动有趣，直观形象。中、高年级的教学注重培养学生的积极思维能力和语言生成能力。

教育部颁发的英语课程标准要求学校从三年级起开设英语课程。不少地方，尤其是沿海经济比较发达的地区，一般都从一年级起开设英语课程。小学是学生学习英语的入门阶段，小学生对英语学习的态度在很大程度上是由兴趣决定的。小学英语课堂教学的特点是活动多、趣味性强、教学过程轻松愉快。这对激发儿童对英语的好奇心，使其对学习英语产生兴趣，并持续喜爱学习英语至关重要。

第二节　英语课程标准的要求

外语是基础教育阶段的必修课程，英语是小学外语课程中的主要语种。英语课程标准由中华人民共和国教育部制定，为英语课程设定课程目标、制定内容标准，是实施教学活动、落实评价机制、开发课程资源、编写英语教材的依据，也是英语课堂教学设计的依据。《义务教育英语课程标准（2022 年版）》强化了课程育人导向，优化了课程内容结构，研制了学业质量标准，增强了指导性，加强了学段衔接。英语教师要清晰地了解英语课程的性质与理念、核心素养的内涵与目标、课程的内容标准和教学要求；知道不同学段的学生在主题、语篇、语言知识、文化知识、语言技能和学习策略等方面应达到的基本要求；把握各年级教学内容、教学要求及相互衔接的关系。

依据《义务教育英语课程标准（2022 年版）》的要求，学生通过英语课程的学习，应达到以下目标：

（1）发展语言能力。能够在感知、体验、积累和运用等语言实践活动中，认识英语与汉语的异同，逐步形成语言意识，积累语言经验，进行有意义的沟通与交流。

（2）培育文化意识。能够了解不同国家的优秀文明成果，比较中外文化的异同，发展跨文化沟通与交流的能力，形成健康向上的审美情趣和正确的价值观；加深对中华文化的理解和认同，树立国际视野，坚定文化自信。

（3）提升思维品质。能够在语言学习中发展思维，在思维发展中推进语言学习；初步从多角度观察和认识世界、看待事物，有理有据、有条理地表达观点；逐步发展逻辑思维、辩证思维和创新思维，使思维体现一定的敏捷性、灵活性、创造性、批判性和深刻性。

（4）提高学习能力。能够树立正确的英语学习目标，保持学习兴趣，主动参与语言实践活动；在学习中注意倾听、乐于交流、大胆尝试；学会自主探究，合作互助；学会反思和评价学习进展，调整学习方式；学会自我管理，提高学习效率，做到乐学善学。

英语课程标准采用国际通用的分级方式，将义务教育阶段英语课程分为三个学段，各学段目标设有相应的级别，一级建议为3～4年级学段应达到的目标，二级建议为5～6年级学段应达到的目标，三级建议为7～9年级学段应达到的目标。各学段目标之间具有联系性、顺序性和进阶型。小学生在结束小学阶段学习时，应达到第二级的学段目标。

英语课程标准在语言能力、文化意识、思维品质和学习能力四个核心素养的二级目标描述如下：

语言能力三个方面的表现如下：

（1）感知与积累。

能领悟基本语调表达的意义；能理解常见词语的意思，理解基本句式和常用时态表达的意义；能通过听，理解询问个人信息的基本表达方式；能听懂日常学习和生活中简单的指令、对话、独白和小故事等；能理解日常生活中用所学语言直接传递的交际意图；能读懂语言简单、主题相关的简短语篇，获取具体信息，理解主要内容。

（2）习得与建构。

在听或看发音清晰、语速适中、句式简单的音视频材料时，能获取有关人物、时间、地点、事件等基本信息；能识别常见语篇类型及其结构；能理解交流个人喜好、情感的表达方式；能根据图片，口头描述其中的人或事物；能关注生活中或媒体上的语言使用。

（3）表达与交流。

能围绕相关主题，运用所学语言，与他人进行简单的交流，表演小故事或短剧，语音、语调基本正确；在书面表达中，能围绕图片内容或模仿范文，写出几句意思连贯的话。

文化意识三个方面的表现如下：

（1）比较与判断。

对学习、探索中外文化有兴趣；能在教师引导下，通过故事、介绍、对话、动画等获取中外文化的简单信息；感知与体验文化多样性，能在理解的基础上进行初步的比较；能用简短的句子描述所学的与中外文化有关的具体事物；初步具有观察、识别、比较中外文化异同的能力。

（2）调适与沟通。

对开展跨文化沟通与交流有兴趣；能与他人友好相处；能在教师引导下，了解不同文化背景下人们待人接物的礼仪；能注意到跨文化沟通与交流中彼此的文化差异；能在人际交往中，尝试理解对方的感受，知道应当规避的谈话内容，适当调整表达方式，体现出礼貌、得体与友善。

（3）感悟与内化。

对了解中外文化有兴趣；能在教师引导下，尝试欣赏英语歌曲、韵文的音韵节奏；能理解与中外优秀文化有关的图片、短文，发现和感悟其中蕴含的人生哲理；有将语言学习与做人、做事相结合的意识和行动；体现爱国主义情怀和文化自信。

思维品质三个方面的表现如下：

（1）观察与辨析。

能对获取的语篇信息进行简单的分类和对比，加深对语篇意义的理解；能比较语篇中的人物、行为、事物或观点间的相似性和差异性，并作出正确的价值判断；能从不同角度辩证地看待事物，学会换位思考。

（2）归纳与推断。

能识别、提炼、概括语篇的关键信息、主要内容、主题意义和观点；能就语篇的主题意义和观点作出正确的理解和判断；能根据语篇推断作者的态度和观点。

（3）批判与创新。

能就作者的观点或意图发表看法，说明理由，交流感受；能对语篇内容进行简单的续编或改编等；具有问题意识，能初步进行独立思考。

学习能力三个方面的表现如下：

（1）乐学与善学。

对英语学习有较浓厚的兴趣和自信心；能积极参与课堂活动，注意倾听，大胆尝试用英语进行交流；乐于参与英语实践活动，遇到问题积极请教，不畏困难。

（2）选择与调整。

能在教师指导下，制订并完成简单的英语学习计划，及时预习和复习所学内容；能了解自己英语学习中的进步与不足；能在教师指导下，初步找到适合自己的英语学习方法；尝试根据学习进展调整学习计划和策略；能借助多种渠道或资源学习英语。

（3）合作与探究。

能在学习活动中与他人合作，共同完成学习任务；能在学习过程中认真思考，主动探究，尝试通过多种方式发现并解决语言学习中的问题。

通过学习和研究英语课程标准，教师可以清晰了解英语课程标准的性质、理念、目标、内容、学业质量以及实施建议，把握不同学段学生应达到的基本要求，使之真正落实到自己的教学实践与评价机制中。

第三节　不同版本教材的内容分析

教材是落实英语课程标准最主要的载体，是英语教学活动中最重要、最核心的教学资源。因此，英语教师要对教材进行深入细致的分析，领会教材编写的意图，了解教材的教学目标，把握教材核心知识内容的前后联系与要求。

小学英语教材版本很多。人民教育出版社就有《新版英语》、《英语》(PEP 版)、《英语》(灵通版)、《英语》(新起点版) 等等。《英语》(牛津版) 有沪教版和苏教版。沪教版小学《英语》(牛津版) 根据上海市小学只开设五个年级，六年级开设在初中的实际情况，分上海本地版和全国版。各省市有各自的《英语》版本，如川教版、湘教版、豫教版、冀教版、鲁教版、浙教版、陕教版、广州版、广东版、深港版、深圳双语版、深圳朗文版、外研社版、北师大版、清华大学版、译林版、仁爱版等，不下几十种。有自主编写的，也有与国外或境外出版机构合作编写的。不同版本的小学英语教材有不同的特色，综合起来，可以归纳出以下几点：

1. 教材编写充分体现课程标准规定的教学目标和要求

教材按照课程标准规定的教学目标和要求编写，主题、语篇、语言知识、文化知识、语言技能和学习策略六个要素共同构成核心要素发展的内容基础。内容和目标相互结合、相互渗透、相互支持，为小学生提供了符合他们心理和生理特点，具有生活性、时代性和文化性的课程内容。教材不仅使学生掌握英语语音、词汇、语法、功能、话题等语言基础知识和听、说、读、写等基本能力，同时也帮助他们掌握科学的学习方法，养成良好的学习习惯，增强学习外语的欲望和自信心，树立团队合作意识和开放意识。

比如人教版小学《英语》(PEP 版) 的内容编排充分考虑到小学生的年龄特征和心理特点，教学内容贴近儿童生活，活动与练习的形式注重儿童智力多元发展，要求学生眼、耳、口、手、脑并用。

三年级第一册 Unit 3 Look at Me 中 A 部分的核心内容是 Let's learn，以下是教材的节选内容：

Look at me.

This is my head.

This is my ear.

This is my eye.

This is my nose.

This is my face.

This is my mouth.

活动有 Let's do，Let's draw，Let's sing：

Touch your head.

Touch your nose.

Touch your eye.

Touch your mouth.

Touch your ear.

Touch your face.

Teddy Bear

Teddy Bear，Teddy Bear，touch your nose.

Teddy Bear，Teddy Bear，turn around.

Teddy Bear，Teddy Bear，touch your head.

Teddy Bear，Teddy Bear，touch the ground.

这些活动都是围绕 Let's learn 中的核心词汇 head，ear，eye，nose，face，mouth 展开的，有听指令做动作、画画、唱歌，既符合小学生的学习特点，又便于教师组织开展教学活动。

B 部分的编排与 A 部分相似，核心内容也是 Let's learn，以下是教材的节选内容：

Finger，body，leg，foot，hand，arm.

活动有 Let's do：

Clap your hands.

Snap your fingers.

Wave your arms.

Cross your legs.

Shake your body.

Stamp your foot.

活动还有 Let's check，听指令选出正确的图片。

活动还有 Let's chant.

—Where is your hand?　　—Here it is.

—Where is your ear?　　—Here it is.

—Where is your mouth?　　—Here it is.

C 部分的内容是 Story time，以下是教材的节选内容：

—Let's make a puppet.

—Good idea.

—First, make the head. Then, make the body.

—Look! Arms and legs.

—Let's play with the puppet. Oh, no! Don't go away.

文化意识接触到 Halloween：

—Happy Halloween!

—Trick or treat! Thank you! Happy Halloween!

还有歌曲 Head, Shoulders, Knees and Toes。

这三个部分的内容层层递进，充分体现了英语课程标准对主题、语篇、语言知识、文化知识、语言技能和学习策略等各个方面的要求。

2. 教学内容紧密联系学生的学习与生活

各版本的教材都是依据教育部制定的英语课程标准中构成核心素养发展的六个要素而编写的，所以尽管版本不同，主题、语篇、语言知识、文化知识、语言技能和学习策略等内容都与学生的学习与生活息息相关。主题为学生学习语言提供语境，语篇为学生提供多样化的文体素材，语言知识提供语言要素，文化知识提供人文内容资源，语言技能有助于学生获取信息、建构知识、表达思想、交流情感，学习策略有利于学生提高学习效率、提升学习效果。

比如主题包括人与自我、人与社会、人与自然三大范畴。个人情况、身体部位、家庭、学校、朋友、数字、形状、时间、天气、季节、颜色、服装、食品、玩具、动植物、日常生活、文体活动、节日等主题都属于这三大范畴。在人教版小学《英语》(新起点版)的目录中，有 School, Body, Animal, Numbers, Colours, Fruit, Toys, Shapes, Clothes, Food and Drink, Family, Friends, Festivals, Seasons, Weather, Time, Myself, Sports and Games, Daily Life 等课题。在冀教版小学《英语》的目录中，有 About Me, My Friends, My School, My Family, Food I Like, My Body, My Day, Animals We Know, Days and Months, Sports, Christmas, Spring Festival 等课题。各种版本的教材内容不仅涵盖了英语课程标准语言知识部分二级目标中的话题，还有 My Room, My Classes, Safety, Jobs, Hobbies, Transport, Nature, People and Countries, Communication, Feelings, Trips, Health, Shopping, The World 等其他相关话题。教材以话题为核心、以功能和结构为主线，教师以任务型活动为目标安排各单元或各课的教学，这可以让学生通过感知、体验、实践、参与、合作等不同方式完成任务，感受成功的愉悦。

3. 递进式编排符合外语学习的客观规律

教材内容和教学要求体现了循序渐进的编写原则，语言材料的呈现由易到难，由浅入深，循序渐进，逐步过渡。教学内容重点突出，难点分散，生词合理复现，便于学生掌握。

比如上海本地版《英语》（牛津版），一至五年级的上册和下册各有四个模块，上册的四个模块分别是：

Module 1 Getting to know you

Module 2 Me，my family and friend

Module 3 Places and activities

Module 4 The natural world

下册的四个模块分别是：

Module 1 Using my five senses

Module 2 My favourite things

Module 3 Things around us

Module 4 More things to learn

也就是说，同一模块的话题会在各个年级反复出现，内容由浅入深，螺旋上升，要求不断提高。

一年级下册的第三个模块 Things around us 中 Unit 1 Seasons 的内容是：

Spring is warm.

Summer is hot.

Autumn is cool.

Winter is cold.

二年级下册的同一模块中 Unit 1 The four seasons 的内容是：

Spring，spring，nice and warm，

Spring，spring，I like spring.

Summer，summer，sunny and hot，

Summer，summer，I like summer.

Autumn，autumn，windy and cool，

Autumn，autumn，I like autumn.

Winter，winter，cloudy and cold，

Winter，winter，I like winter.

三年级下册的同一模块中 Unit 1 Seasons 的内容是：

In spring，it is warm.

We can plant trees.

We can have picnics in the park.

In summer，it is hot.

We can go to the beach.

We can swim and make sandcastles there.

In autumn，it is cool.

We can fly kites and ride bicycles in the park.

In winter，it is cold.

We have hats，gloves and scarves.

We can ice-skate. It's fun.

可以看出，同样的话题，随着年级的增长，内容在逐渐加深，知识在不断拓展，要求在不断提高。这样的编排符合小学生的学习规律，给学生的学习架构了坡度，话题的复现降低了学生学习的难度，提高了学生学习的效率。

4. 丰富的教学活动激发学生求知欲望

各版本教材内容的选择与安排充分考虑到小学生的兴趣、爱好、愿望等学习需求和心理需求，材料趣味性强，话题鲜活，体裁多样，这足以激发学生的学习动机，使其形成积极的学习态度。

比如上海本地版《英语》（牛津版）每个单元不仅包括单词学习和句型学习这两个呈现核心词汇与句型的栏目，还设置了角色扮演活动、游戏活动、调查活动、拓展阅读、问答练习、语音学习、故事欣赏、童谣和歌曲、画图并描述等栏目。丰富多彩的教学活动可以减轻学生的学习压力，激发他们的学习兴趣与求知欲，使学习变得轻松愉快。活动的合理安排还能帮助学生养成良好的学习习惯，形成有效的学习方法，发展自主学习的能力，为他们今后的进一步学习和可持续发展打下基础。

5. 教科书与配套参考资料的开放性有利于不同学力学生英语能力的提高

我国幅员辽阔，发展水平参差不齐。即使是在同一地区、同一城市，各学校的师资、生源、客观条件的差异也很大。考虑到学校差异、教师差异和学生个体差异对外语学习的影响，教材在教学内容的安排上需具有一定的灵活性。教材除了包含课程标准规定要掌握的内容以外，还提供一定数量的拓展内容，供教师和学生选择使用。比如小学《英语》（PEP 版）每单元按 A、B、C 三个大课型设计，C 部分是供选择的教学内容。教师在保证完成教学基本目标的前提下，可以根据本地区的课时和自己教学的实际情况，灵活调整教学内容和学习进度，以满足不同层次学生的需求，使所有的学生在语言知识和语言能力上均有所发展。这在一定程度上改变了以往教材在教学内容上“一刀切”的状况，留出了一定的弹性内容，使教师能够充分发挥特长，使学生能够各得其所，满足了学生个性发展的需求。

对于教学参考资料中的教学建议，教师可以根据各自不同的教学需求，创造性地、个性化地选择开展教学活动。如果认为某项活动难度太高，教师可以不选，也可以自主扩展活动的步骤，增加准备性或提示性的活动，以降低活动难度。如果活动太容易，教师可以放弃，也可以增加难度或进行延伸。根据实际教学情况调整方法与步骤可以达到因材施教的目的，使不同的学生都得到发展。

教师参考资料还为教师提供了灵活多样的教学评价建议，如采用终结性评价与形成性评价相结合的方式。终结性评价是在教学活动结束后为判断其效果而进行的评价，形式有期中、期末考试。形成性评价贯穿于整个教学过程，教师可随时了解学生的日常学习的情况，形式有课堂学习活动评比、学习效果自评、学习档案、问卷调查、访谈、家长对学生学习情况的反馈与评价等等。建议教师根据学生的年龄特征和学习风格的差异采用适当的评价方式，使评价机制更公平合理，更能客观反映学生的实际学习情况。

第四节　教学设计的要求

小学英语教学设计要符合小学生的生理、心理特点，创设良好的语言环境，组织生动活泼的课堂教学活动，使学生在愉快自信的情绪中学习，在大量的语言实践中形成语感，养成良好的语言学习习惯。具体要求如下：

1. 激发学生学习兴趣

教师在教学设计时要注重培养学生的学习兴趣，并保持他们的注意力。教师要营造积极的课堂生态，创设宽松、平等、和谐的课堂氛围，引导学生注意倾听，大胆表达。兴趣是积极的情绪表现，是内在的动力因素。为了激发学生的学习兴趣，教师可以在教学中结合教学内容设计安排一些游戏、歌曲、童谣、角色扮演等教学活动，避免枯燥的语言知识讲解和死记硬背，寓教于乐，使学习变得轻松愉快，使学生喜欢学、乐意学，从而取得事半功倍的效果。

2. 确保学生主体地位

教师在教学设计时要充分尊重学生的主体地位，切忌从自己的角度出发安排教学活动。要面向全体学生，从学生的实际情况出发，努力使每个学生都参与教学活动。学生个体的学习能力不同，教师对他们的要求也应有变化。对学习能力强的学生，要求可以高一些，对学习能力不那么高的学生，要求可以降低些。师生的互动不仅有单向的，也有双向的、网状的、多种形式的，以确保人人都有练习机会，都能得到发展和提高。

3. 符合语言学习规律

教师在教学设计中要遵循外语学习的规律，循序渐进，要考虑到学生学习外语会受到母语的影响，错误是难免的，所以不能急于求成。安排学生学习的内容要符合学生认知规律，从体验、模仿到理解、应用，从直观到抽象，从单项到综合，由浅入深，由易及难。

句型操练先短后长，先机械后灵活。视听说领先，读写跟上，使学生听、说、读、写的能力都得到发展。

4. 体现语言交际功能

学习语言的最终目的是使用语言。教师在教学设计中要利用各种教学手段和资源，为学生创设情境，使学习有意义，使学生学习的语言是实际有用的。操练是必须的，但只有机械操练是不够的。教师组织的教学活动要贴近学生的学习生活，体现学生想要表达的内容。尽量避免问无意义的问题，造无使用价值的句子，充分体现形式、意义和使用统一的原则。

5. 巧妙使用激励机制

小学生好胜心强，喜欢比赛、竞争。教师在教学设计中可以利用这一特点，开展多种形式的竞赛活动，并融入过程评价机制。竞赛活动不仅能活跃课堂气氛，鼓励学生积极思考，积极参与，还能增强学生的荣誉感和团队合作精神。在竞赛活动中，教师采取以激励为主的评价方式，给予学生充分的鼓励和肯定，并将其记入学生的平时成绩，这可以提高学生的成就感和自信心。

6. 重视指导学习方法

科学的学习方法有助于提升学生的学习效率。教师要重视指导学生的学习方法，帮助不同年龄阶段的学生，根据不同的实际需求，选择适当的学习方法，完成学习任务，解决学习中出现的问题，逐步形成适合自己的学习策略。比如，课前布置预习内容，要有明确的要求，课后布置复习内容，要有可操作性。根据教学内容提供拼读规则，帮助学生记忆单词。每个模块学习结束后，梳理归纳所学内容，发现问题，及时解决。鼓励学生课外自主拓展学习，真正做到乐学、善学。

教案设计

本章导读

上课前要准备，要有教学方案。怎么备课？教案怎么设计？要包含哪些要素？要解决哪些问题？如果需要在很短的时间内设计教案，有什么方法？本章会一一回答这些问题，并介绍一些微格教案。

教案也称为课时计划，是教学设计的核心部分，是完成教学任务、保证教学质量的重要条件，是培养教师教学技能的重要途径。教案的设计应该建立在了解掌握英语课程标准和小学英语学科特点的基础上。教师在分析、领会、消化教材内容后再对其进行重构，使之贴合教学对象的需求。教案设计要求教师对课堂教学进行科学有效的安排，形成一个优化的方案，使学生在有限的课时内学到更多的知识，掌握更多的技能。教案的形成是一个创新的过程，也是教学设计的具体体现。

教案设计的格式不尽相同，归纳起来，应该包含课题，课型，授课日期，授课对象，本课时或本单元的教学目标、教学内容、教学重点和难点、教学资源的应用、教学过程与方法、设计意图和时间分配、作业布置、板书设计、课后的教学反思等内容。

第一节　设定教学目标

英语课程标准的总目标是发展语言能力、培育文化意识、提升思维品质、提高学习能力。教师在这个总体目标的指导下，设定课堂教学目标。课堂教学目标比课程目标具体，是课程目标在具体的教学过程中的体现。教师根据课程目标、教材内容和学生情况，参考教师用书的建议，确定某一单元或某一课时的具体目标。教学目标有三个维度：知识与技能、过程与方法、情感态度与价值观。知识与技能目标是对学生学习结果的描述，即学生通过学习所达到的结果，也称为结果性目标。这种目标一般有学懂、学会和能应用三个层次的要求。过程与方法目标是学生在教师的指导下获取知识与技能的程序和具体做法，即让学生学会发现问题、思考问题、解决问题，学会学习，拥有创新精神和实践能力。它是过程中的目标，又称程序性目标。这种目标强调做中学、学中做和反思三个过程。情感态度与价值观目标是让学生形成积极的学习态度、健康向上的人生态度，具有科学精神和正确的世界观、人生观、价值观。情感不仅指学习兴趣、学习热情、学习动机，更指内心体验和心灵世界的丰富。态度不仅指学习态度、学习责任，更指乐观的生活态度、求实的科学态度和宽容的人生态度。价值观不仅强调个人价值，更强调个人价值与社会价值的统一，不仅强调科学价值，更强调科学价值与人文价值的统一，不仅强调人类价值，更强调人类价值与自然价值的统一，从而使学生从内心确立起对真善美的价值追求以及人与自然和谐、可持续发展的理念。情感态度与价值观目标是学生对学习过程和结果的主观经验，也就是体验学习过程和结果后的倾向和感受，也称体验性目标。这种目标有认同、体会和内化三个层次。根据以上描述，教师在设定课堂教学目标时要注意以下几点：

1. 注重教学目标的全面性

注重教学目标的全面性就是要充分考虑教学目标三个维度的各个方面。设定教学目标时，要把三个维度作为一个整体来考虑。知识与技能目标是过程与方法目标、情感态度与价值观目标的基础，过程与方法目标是实现知识与技能目标的载体，情感态度与价值观目标对其他目标有重要的促进和优化作用。三者是一个有机的整体，是同一事物的三个方面。三个维度互相照应，相互协调，体现高度的整合作用。知识与技能维度的目标立足于让学生学会，过程与方法维度的目标立足于让学生会学，情感态度与价值观维度的目标立足于让学生乐学。任何割裂知识与技能、过程与方法、情感态度与价值观三维目标的教学都不能促进学生的健康全面发展。

知识与技能目标是过程与方法目标、情感态度与价值观目标的基础，只有落实知识与技能目标，才能实现其他目标。在设定知识与技能目标时，教师一定要突出英语的核心词汇与句型，使学生在理解和掌握这些知识点的同时，掌握听、说、读、写的能力。把过程与方法作为教学目标，是新课改的一大亮点。教学要重视结果，更要重视过程与方法。过程与方法目标要体现学生的学习过程和思维过程。情感态度与价值观目标是在原有德育目标基础上的进一步明确和提升，主要是让学生体验英语在现实生活中的价值和意义。

2. 注重教学目标的准确性

在设定教学目标时，要注意语言表述的准确性，避免使用“初步理解”“基本掌握”这类含糊的词语。目标描述的行为主体是学生，如果用“使学生”“培养学生”等词语，行为主体就变成了教师。如果要表达教师行为，可以用“在教师的指导下”“帮助下”“引导下”等词语。英语课程标准中对语言知识目标的描述用了“了解”“理解”“学会”“运用”等表示不同层面的词语，对语言技能目标的表述都用“能”。以上都是将学生作为行为主体来描述的。

3. 注重教学目标的可操作性

教学目标的作用在于具体地指导教学实践。要让教学目标发挥最大的功效，就要将教学目标设计得细致、具体，也就是要有可操作性。教学目标的设计属于课前准备，是对课堂教学的预设，预设的结果将直接影响课堂教学的效果。教学目标定得太笼统、太空泛、太模糊，就会失去教学目标的实际指导作用。不具有可操作性的教学目标就只能成为一种空洞的摆设，课堂教学就不会取得预期效果。而预设的目标越是具体明晰，指导性也就越强，课堂教学的效果也就越好。因此，在教学目标设计中，一定要注重可操作性。为了有效提高教学目标的可操作性，教师要尽可能选用意义明确、易于理解的词语。比如了解层面上常用的有“学习”“知道”“识别”“辨认”等，理解层面上常用的有“学会”“听懂”“领悟”“掌握”等，应用层面上常用的有“选择”“判断”“翻译”“运用”等。

4. 注重教学目标的合理性

三维目标的达成是一个渐进的螺旋上升的过程，不可能一蹴而就，想通过一节课或一个单元的教学就完全达成各项目标是不现实的。即使是知识与技能中的某些具体目标，也有一个从识记到理解到运用的过程，也不可能刚学习就能被掌握运用。有些教学目标，尤其是涉及过程与方法的目标、情感态度与价值观的目标，应该是一个在原有基础上不断提高的过程，甚至是整个基础教育阶段的任务，是长期教育的任务。每一堂课都应该融入三维目标的理念，但这并不意味要在一堂课的时间内，同时落实非常具体的三维目标。教师应该在达成知识与技能这一外在目标的同时，逐步达成过程与方法、情感态度与价值观等内在目标。

第二节　确立重点难点

教师在进行教学设计时，要对教材进行深入的研究和细致的分析。这不是针对某一课时或某一单元，而是要对整个学期、整个年段，甚至整个学段的总体目标有清晰的认识。在对单元进行设计时，要明确教材的主要教学内容、教学的重点与难点，针对学生的实际学习能力、不同学生的不同特点和需求，对教材所提供的材料进行合理的整合加工，可以适当增加或删减，以学生的发展为出发点用好教材。

1. 语音教学中的重点难点

语音教学中的难点在于一些汉语中没有的读音，比如字母 a 在闭音节中的读音/æ/，

th 在单词中的读音/θ/或/ð/，sh 在单词中的读音/ʃ/，ch 在单词中的读音/tʃ/，浊辅音/ʒ/和/dʒ/，集中双元音/ɪə/、/ɛə/和/ʊə/等等。学生从未接触过这些读音，所以不易掌握。还有一些音素的读音与汉语的读音有相似之处，但容易混淆。比如/ɪ/在英语中是元音音素，发音时舌尖抵下齿，舌前部向硬腭抬起，而学生受汉语“衣”的读音影响，舌前部与硬腭形成一定的阻碍，发成英语/jɪ/的读音。/ɑː/在英语中是后元音，但学生受到汉语在语音方面的负迁移影响，发成汉语中的“ɑ”的读音，舌位很靠前。像这些难点就应该作为教学的重点。

前元音/e/与/æ/的读音也容易混淆，发/æ/时，舌尖抵住下齿，舌前部降低，牙床近乎全开，上下齿间可容纳食指和中指两指相叠平放的宽度，双唇近全开且扁平。但学生往往不能将其与/e/加以区别而发成相似的音，或以/ɛ/替代/e/和/æ/。/ɛ/在英语语音里不单独成为一个音素，它是英国语音学家丹尼尔·琼斯（Daniel Jones）为了更加精确地描写一种语言里元音的读音，区别不同语言里相似的元音，确定各个元音读音的具体舌位而研究设计的名为“基本元音”系统中的一个元音。发/ɛ/时，口腔张开度与舌位高低都介于/e/与/æ/之间，其发音又与汉语“ie”中“e”的发音相似，学生容易混淆，所以发/e/时开口度大了，发/æ/时开口度又小了，结果/e/和/æ/都成了/ɛ/。

英语在连贯表达时，音的长度、单词与句子的重音、音调的高低起伏等超音段特征是话语信息传递的重要表现形式，它们的相互作用使话语具有特殊的语义功能，也是表达说话人的态度或情绪的重要方式，但对初学英语的小学生来说这是较难理解的。在言语表达中，音与音之间的长度是有区别的，元音比辅音读得长，双元音没有长音符号，但要与长元音读得一样长。重音分单词重音和句子重音，单词重音比较容易掌握，句子重音则不易掌握。英语属于语调语言，汉语属于声调语言。中国学生已习惯汉语语句表达方式，受母语负迁移影响，朗读英语时倾向把重音平均分配到每个单词，破坏了英语的节奏感和特有的韵律，说来非常不自然。在英语连贯表达中，一些词语会因为语义的重要性、强调作用、节奏等保留重音，另一些词语则失去了重音，这些保留下来的重音构成句子重音。语句中重读音节基本在相等的时距中出现，以其重、轻相间形成节奏。由于名词、实义动词、形容词、副词、数词等实词保留了重音且语速较慢，介词、冠词、连词、人称代词等虚词失去了重音且语速较快，句子关键词的意思更为突出，便于理解。同样的句子，由于句子重音不同，意思大相径庭。比如 You should stick the stamp on yourself. On 在这里是副词，应该重读，句子解释为“你应当自己把邮票贴上去”。如果 on 失去了重音，句子的意思就变成“你应当把邮票贴在你自己身上”，这岂不闹笑话。

在语调中，学生较难掌握的是升调。语句最后一个重读音节的升或降决定句子的语调，表达说话者不同的语气、态度及观点，有很强的语义功能，有助于听话者了解句子的意思和说话者的态度，并更好地获得交际中的信息。Pardon 用不同的语调表达，意思也不一样：用升调表示“请再说一遍”，用降调表示“请你原谅”。这些重点和难点，需要教师在教学中格外重视，只对单个音素的正确发音过分注意而忽视其在特定语境中的变异，会给学生的口语表达带来问题，英语听来会非常不自然。教师要想方设法解决学生在外语学习中由于负迁移作用所造成的问题，及时发现学生在语音学习中遇到的困难，并针对问题探索相应对策。模仿是最有效的教学方法，教师要充分利用教学技术与资源，为小学生提供各种喜闻乐见的视听材料，供小学生模仿和实践，帮助他们养成良好的发音习惯。

2. 词汇教学中的重点难点

词汇教学是小学英语教学中最基本的内容之一。英语课程标准二级目标要求学生能初步运用500个左右的单词，就规定的主题进行交流与表达。这些主题涉及的词汇都是表达数字、颜色、时间、天气、食品、服装、玩具、动植物、身体部位、个人情况、家庭、学校、朋友、文体活动、节日等英语中最基本最常用的词汇，大多为名词和动词。在词汇教学中要解决音、形、义和用的问题。比如学习单词 bread，要会读/bred/，会拼写 b-r-e-a-d bread，知道它的意思是面包，而且在你想要面包时能用句型 I want 来表达，并在 bread 前面加上 some，以表示这是个不可数名词。例如，I want some bread.

在这四会中，单词音和义的教学可以结合起来。比如单词 book 的教学，教师可以在出示书本的同时，让学生听这个单词的读音/buk/，并让其跟读，发现学生有发音错误及时纠正。在学生掌握了单词的读音后，教师可以教授单词的拼写，即单词的形。单词的拼写是教学的难点，学生常常会感到记忆单词有困难。英语是表音文字，读音与拼写之间存在一定的关系，也就是读音规律。在学生学习国际音标前，教师在教学中要有计划、逐步地使学生了解字母和字母组合在单词中的读音，音形结合，培养学生借助字母和字母组合的读音规则来拼读单词的能力，帮助学生解决记忆单词的困难。

3. 语法教学中的重点难点

小学英语教材一般不出现显性语法教学的内容，取而代之的是体现在句型教学中的，通过句型操练，帮助学生掌握英语课程标准语法二级的知识内容：理解常用简单句的基本结构和表意功能；理解一般过去时与一般将来时的形式、意义、用法；运用所学语法知识描述、比较人和物；描述具体事件的发生、发展和结局，描述时间、地点和方位等。

名词的单复数形式是学生学习的难点。在汉语的表达中，比如一个学生和两个学生，学生两个字是没有变化的。英语则不同，名词有单复数之分。例如，One student，two students. 复数名词的形式是在单数名词的词尾加上 s（大多数情况）。这对法国学生、德国学生来说不是问题，因为法语和德语的语法也有类似形式，而且更复杂，它们的名词还有阴阳性之分。但汉语是没有这种变化的，学生要克服母语的负迁移作用是很困难的，不要说小学生，即使是中学生，甚至是大学生，也难免经常犯这种低级错误。

动词的形式变化也是学生学习的难点。英语动词有时态的变化，动作和状况发生的时间不同，动词的形式也不同。比如动词“come”：

He came here yesterday.

He has been here.

He has come here.

He is coming here.

He will come here tomorrow.

在汉语中，“去”是不变的，时间的变化体现在其他词上：

他昨天来这儿了。

他来过这儿了。

他已经来这儿了。

他正在来这儿的路上。

他明天来这儿。

不管是名词的单复数，还是动词的形式变化，改变多年来养成的汉语思维习惯不是一蹴而就的，教师应有打持久战的思想准备。除了运用形象的直观手法加深学生的印象，教师还要在整个小学阶段的英语教学过程中不断强调，让学生逐步克服母语的负迁移影响，理解和养成汉英表达的不同习惯。

第三节 安排教学过程

安排教学过程就是设计课堂教学流程，是实施教学任务的重要步骤。一般的程序有准备环节、呈现环节、操练环节、应用环节和结课环节。

(1) 准备环节主要是热身，激活学生的大脑和行动，让学生兴奋起来，即激发兴趣，烘托学习氛围。热身阶段的活动形式有唱歌、念诗、做游戏、讲故事、表演、角色扮演、日常交流、问答活动、复述课文、专题汇报等等。教师在选择活动形式时，一定要根据自己的教学实际，选择适合学生和教学内容的活动，以求实效。准备环节的时间不宜太长，大概 3～5 分钟。

(2) 呈现环节是语言输入的最初阶段，教师根据教材的内容和学生的实际情况，灵活地选择呈现方式，比如图片、挂图、录音、VCD、投影、绘画、表演、歌曲、歌谣、游戏、故事、小品、头脑风暴、设问等等。新的学习内容可以由教师来呈现，也可以由学生配合教师共同来呈现，还可以在教师的指导下，由学生个人结对或小组形式来呈现。时间大致在 5～10 分钟，教师要根据教学的实际情况来灵活调整时间。

(3) 学生在通过呈现环节基本了解了本堂课主要学习的内容后进入操练环节。在操练环节中，教师组织学生参与大量的、不同形式的活动进行操练，帮助学生内化语言，并为语言的输出打下扎实的基础。操练的方法有替换练习、问答交流、游戏、歌谣、歌曲、表演、对话角色扮演、故事表演、短剧表演、绘画与交流、制作与交流等等。操练方法的选择会直接影响到操练效果，教师要根据不同学段的学生情况，根据实际的教学内容来选择最适合自己教学实际的语言操练方法。操练环节是学生学习和掌握语言的关键环节，它起着承上启下的重要作用。时间至少需要 15 分钟。教师也可以根据自己的教学实际灵活安排时间，也可以将呈现和操练这两个环节有机地整合在一起进行教学。

（4）在应用环节中，教师通常用布置任务的形式，使学生应用所学的语言知识，展示所掌握的语言技能，也就是让学生用所学的语言去做事，去完成真实任务或模拟真实任务，以达到语言输出的目的。教师在布置任务时，应当充分考虑到学生在实施任务、解决问题的过程中，需要应用哪些基本词汇、句型和日常套语，会涉及哪些相关的语言知识，还能复习哪些已经学过的语言知识，并为所需情境进行必要的空间布置。时间大致在 5～10 分钟。教师也可以结合实际情况灵活安排时间。

（5）结课环节出现在一堂课即将结束时。教师用 3～5 分钟时间归纳总结所学的语言知识，评价学生在各项学习活动中的表现和实际效果，布置作业。作业的设计要考虑它的有效性、可操作性和可检测性。不应为布置作业而布置作业，或只布置抄写或默写单词、句型、对话和课文等抽象记忆语言知识的作业。应当把作业的内容视为课堂教学的延续，注意口头作业与书面作业的结合、语言知识与语言技能的结合。对小学阶段低年级学生，可以布置一些听做、说唱、玩演等用所学语言与他人简单交流的作业，对中高年级学生，可在低年级的基础上，增加读、写的作业。

教师在安排教学过程的同时，除了可以充分利用课程提供的教材、练习册、教师参考书、教学挂图等文本资源，还可以结合教学需要，开发和利用实物、学具、教具、课件、光盘、网络、录音录像资料、广播影视节目等多种资源，拓展学用渠道。

另外，教师还要考虑板书设计。板书设计是教学设计中的画龙点睛之笔，是教师在教学过程中运用文字、符号、图表、简笔画等手段，有效提高教学质量的一种教学行为。作为课堂教学的重要组成部分，板书可以帮助学生把握重点、理清思路、加深印象。除此之外，板书还能帮助教师在教学过程中增强吸引力、感染力和启发性，培养学生的分析能力、概括能力，启发思维。

教师在将教学设计付诸教学实践后，要分析研究其使用效果，进行评价与反思，发现不足，及时修改，使之不断完善。

第四节 如何在短时间内准备教案

教育部制定的《中小学教师资格考试暂行办法》规定：参加教师资格考试合格是教师职业准入的前提条件。申请幼儿园、小学、初级中学、普通高级中学、中等职业学校教师和中等职业学校实习指导教师资格的人员须分别参加相应类别的教师资格考试。教育部教师工作司、教育部考试中心制定的《小学教师资格考试面试大纲（试行）》规定的测试方法是：结构化面试和情境模拟相结合，具体方式有抽题备课、试讲、答辩等。考生按照有关规定随机抽取备课题目，进行试讲。在教学设计方面，考生被要求能够根据课程标准处理教学材料，确定教学目标，突出重点和难点；能够基于小学生的知识基础和生活经验合理设计教学活动；学生活动设计有效，能引导学生通过自主参与、合作探究的方式达成学习目标。在教学实施方面，考生被要求教学结构合理，条理清晰，能较好地控制教学节奏；知识讲授准确，能基本完成教学任务；能根据学生认知特点和学科教学规律，选择恰当的教学方法，有效激发学生的学习动力；能根据教学需要运用教具、学具和现代教育技术辅助教学；板书工整规范、布局合理。在教学评价方面，考生被要求能够采用恰当的评价方式对学生的学习活动做出反馈；能对自己的教学过程进行反思，做出比较客观的评价。

考生在抽到题目后有 20 分钟时间进行教学设计，然后试讲 10 分钟。如何在 20 分钟时间内完成教学设计，在教学实施的 10 分钟内体现呈现、操练、应用环节呢？

1. 看清文本要求，确定教学目标

试讲的教学内容基于小学英语教材。一定要准确理解，杜绝偏差。对题目要求的误解，就像作文跑题，全盘皆输。语言知识方面的要求有语音、词汇、语法（语法在小学阶段是通过句型的形式来显现的）三个方面。语言技能方面的要求有听说和读写，读包括阅读和朗读。小学阶段的英语教学内容浅显，几个单词、一两个句型、一段对话或一段短文。如果是单词与句型，教学重点明确。如果是对话或短文，就要从语篇中找出关键词和难点作为教学重点。了解教学材料的内容，就可以确定教学的重点与难点，也就是要完成的教学任务。

2. 以小学生为本，设计教学活动

在教学任务明确后，要设计完成任务的方法，也就是通过什么教学活动来达成教学目的。教师在设计活动时一定要从学生的角度去考虑问题。尽管教学内容很浅显，但对学生而言是全新的。教学活动要有效、有趣，适合小学生，贴近他们的学习生活。可以设计一些简单、有用的教具，同时考虑板书的内容。

3. 教学结构合理，体现师生互动

虽然试讲的时间只有 10 分钟，但在这 10 分钟内要体现完整的教学过程。教师可以创设情境导入教学内容，根据需要进行句型操练，通过游戏活动了解学生的掌握程度，以布置作业结束试讲。在教学过程中，可以想象面前有一些小学生。这样，教师就可以与想象中的学生互动，请他们参与教学活动，并对他们的表现做出评价。

第五节　微格教学案例

案例1

主题： Body parts

教学目标：

学习有关脸部的单词 eye，nose，mouth，ear，face，能用句型 This is my… 来介绍自己的这些器官。

教学内容：

单词：eye，nose，mouth，ear，face

句型：This is my….

教学过程：

在准备环节，教师可以让学生听 This Is My Face 这首歌，营造轻松的学习气氛，引起学生的学习兴趣。

This Is My Face
Eye and ear,
And mouth and nose,
Mouth and nose,
Mouth and nose.
Eye and ear,
And mouth and nose,
This is my face.

然后，教师通过给学生介绍一个小丑朋友来导入新授内容，利用小丑的脸逐一呈现 face，eye，nose，mouth，ear，要求学生根据教师所指的部位说出单词，并引导学生注意拼写与读音的关系。

教师可以通过各种游戏活动来激发学生的学习积极性，巩固所学的新知识。

1. 指令游戏

当教师说“Touch your nose”，学生要用手碰鼻子。然后变换规则，当教师说“Touch your nose”，学生可以用手碰其他部位，但不能碰鼻子。

2. 指出缺少的器官

教师出示不完整的脸部图片，问学生“What's missing?”要求学生指出缺少的器官。

3. 照镜子游戏

两人一组，学生轮流看着镜子里的自己，用句型 This is my…来介绍自己的器官。

4. 画脸游戏

蒙上学生的眼睛，要求学生根据教师的指令在黑板上的空脸中添上五官。

5. 介绍自己

教师在屏幕上滚动放映学生的头像，停在哪名学生的头像上，就由那名学生来介绍自己的五官。学生还可以运用一些学过的形容词来描述。

案例 2

主题：Animals

教学目标：

学习 bear，panda，tiger，monkey 四个生词和句型 What's this? It's a…。

能简单描述上述四种动物。

教学内容：

单词：bear，panda，tiger，monkey

句型：What's this? It's a….

教学过程：

教师让学生听某一动物的叫声，要求学生猜是什么动物。以此游戏复习已学单词 chick，duck，cow，pig，营造轻松的学习氛围。然后以同样的方法呈现 bear。

Listen to the bear's sound. What's this? Read and spell the word. Read the rhyme：

What's this?

What's this?

It's big.

It's brown.

It's a bear.

通过猜谜语的游戏呈现 tiger。

It is strong.

It is fat.

It is brown and black.

It likes meat.

What's this?

Read and spell the word.

Sing a song：Two Tigers

以听动物的叫声来猜动物的游戏呈现 monkey。

What's this?

Read and spell the word.

Show the students different monkeys' pictures.

What's this?

It's a monkey.

It's thin.

通过猜谜语的游戏呈现 panda。

It's black and white.

It's big and fat.

It's lovely.

It likes bamboos.

What's this?

Where can we see pandas?

教师展示上述四种动物的图片，复习句型 What's this? It's a…。

要求学生介绍他们喜欢的动物。

案例 3

主题：Position

教学目标：

能理解介词 in，on，under，near 的基本含义，并能用这 4 个介词和句型 Where is…? It is…来询问和表示方位。

教学内容：

介词：in，on，under，near

句型：Where is…? It is….

教学过程：

教师利用教室里的实物以问答形式复习单词。

What's this?

It's a pen/pencil/pencil-case/box/desk/chair.

教师把铅笔放进笔袋里，把钢笔放进盒子里，边做边说。

Where is the pencil? It is in the pencil-case. Where is the pen? It is in the box.

在学生理解了 in 的用法后，让他们用 in 造句。然后以相同的方法教 on，under，near。

教师请学生用这 4 个介词画简单的表示物品方位的图画，然后用句型 Where is the…？It is…向全班介绍画中物品的位置。

教师收集学生画的图，抽出其中的一张，不要让学生看见。然后根据画中的物品问 Where is the…？要求学生用 Is it（in/on/under/near）…来猜画中物品的位置，猜中的学生胜出。

案例 4

主题：Shopping

教学目标：

学习购物的基本表达方式，掌握句型 Can I help you? May I have some…？How much?

教学内容：

对话 In the shop

A：Can I help you?

B：Yes，I want some apples.

A：OK. We have many fresh apples here.

B：How much?

A：9 yuan per kilo.

B：I will get 6 apples. And may I have some bananas，please?

A：Of course.

B：How much altogether?

A：19 yuan.

B：Here's 20 yuan.

A：Here's your change. Thank you. Bye!

B：Bye-bye!

教学过程：

教师提问 Do you like apples/oranges/bananas/peaches? 让学生复习水果名称。

然后朗读童谣，复习几种水果的单复数形式和数字：

Two，two，two pears；

Four，four，four apples；

Five，five，five bananas；

Six，six，six oranges；

Let's eat fruits!

教师创设购物环境，让学生听录音。

A：Can I help you?

B：Yes，I want some apples.

A：OK. We have many fresh apples here.

B：How much?

A：9 yuan per kilo.

B：I will get 6 apples. And may I have some bananas，please?

A：Of course.

B：How much altogether?

A：19 yuan.

B：Here's 20 yuan.

A：Here's your change. Thank you. Bye!

B：Bye-bye!

然后分别教授句型并且板书。

Can I help you?

May I have some…?

How much?

在学生掌握这些表达方式后，要求他们运用所学句型，扮演营业员和顾客，根据各自的喜好购买水果。

案例5

主题：Seeing the doctor

教学目标：

学习词组 have a cold，have a cough，have a fever，have a headache，take some medicine 和句型 What should I do? You should…。

能简单描述病症，提出建议。

教学内容：

词组：have a cold，have a cough，have a fever，have a headache，take some medicine

句型：What should I do? You should….

教学过程：

教师结合肢体语言介绍自己的健康状况，导入词组 have a cold，have a cough，have a fever，have a headache。

I don't fell well today. I have a cold. I have a headache. I have a cough. I have a fever.

教师逐一教授以上4个词组，然后让学生说出教师用肢体语言演示的病症。教师创设就诊室的情境，自己扮演医生，请一名学生扮演病人，让其他学生边看边听对话。

Doctor：How do you feel?

Patient：I have a cold. I have a headache. I have a cough. I have a fever.

Doctor：You should take some medicine. You should drink a lot of water. You should have a good rest.

组织学生两人一组操练句型：

What should I do?

You should….

然后让学生扮演医生和病人进行对话。

第三章

准备环节的设计

本章导读

教案设计好了，就可以进课堂实施教学了，但一堂课如何开始呢？这一章将介绍准备环节中要完成的任务，并提供一些可以在这一环节开展的活动。

准备环节也称为热身（warming up）。准备环节的目的是使学生尽快进入积极的学习状态。小学生活泼好动，在下课十分钟内也会奔跑玩耍，有时两分钟预备铃的时间还不能让他们安静下来，所以教师要在上课伊始的三五分钟内进行组织教学，建立课堂教学秩序，稳定学生的情绪，形成良好的英语学习气氛。在组织教学时，教师可以开展一些轻松有趣的启动性活动，比如请学生做值日生报告、唱英语歌、诵读童谣、快速问答等等。这些活动应尽可能与将要学习的内容联系起来。

第一节　问答活动

问答活动是常用的热身方法之一。教师可根据本课时教学内容的需要设定一些问题，要求学生快速反应作答。当然，这些问题应该是学生能回答的。

第 1 组问题

主题： Personal information

Hello! How are you?

What's your name?

What's your last name?

Can you spell it?

How old are you?

How tall are you?

Where are you from?

Where do you live now?

How many people are there in your family?

Do you live with your grandparents?

Do you have brothers or sisters?

第 2 组问题

主题： Cities

What city are you in now?

Where is your home town?

What's the largest city in China?

Where is the capital of China?

Can you tell me a little about your city?

第 3 组问题

主题： Weather and Seasons

How is the weather today?

What's the weather like today?

Is it very hot?

It's sunny，isn't it?

What's the temperature today?

What's your favourite season?

What clothes do you wear in summer?

Which season do you like best?

Why do you like summer best?

第 4 组问题

主题： Numbers

How many people are there in your family?

How many students are there here now?

How many English lessons do you have in a week?

How many days are there in a week?

How many days are there in June?

How many days are there in a year?

How many letters are there in your last name?

第 5 组问题

主题：Time and Daily Activities

What's the time?

What time is it?

Do you get up at six?

What time do you get to school?

When do you go to bed?

What do you usually do on weekends?

第 6 组问题

主题：Days and Dates

What day is it today?

What's the date today?

When is your birthday?

When is our National Day?

When is Children's Day?

When is Christmas?

第 7 组问题

主题：Seeing the Doctor

Do you feel well?

How do you feel today?

What's the matter?

What's wrong?

Can you sleep well?

Do you have a fever?

第 8 组问题

主题：Interests and Hobbies

Do you like English?

Do you like music?

Do you like sports?

What subject do you like most?

Do you like reading?

Who's your favourite singer?

What's your favourite TV program?

What do you usually do after school?

第 9 组问题

主题： Food and Drinks

Do you like fish or meat?

Do you eat a lot of vegetables?

What's your favourite fruit?

Do you like pizza?

Do you drink milk every day?

What do you like to drink?

What do you have for breakfast?

第 10 组问题

主题： Position and Distance

Where's the zoo?

Is it very far?

Is there a bus stop near here?

How far is the subway station?

How can I get to the children's palace?

Can you tell me the way to the shopping centre?

第二节 唱歌活动

唱英语歌曲也常常被英语教师用作热身。教师可以请学生领唱，或请学生指挥全班一起唱。为了使歌词的内容更符合教学要求，教师可以利用现成的曲调，改编歌词或自己填词。

歌曲 1

主题：Family Members

The Finger Family

Daddy Finger，Daddy Finger.
Here I am! Here I am!
How are you today?
Very well，thank you.
Run away. Run away.

Mommy Finger，Mummy Finger.
Here I am! Here I am!
How are you today?
Very well，thank you.
Run away. Run away.

Brother Finger，Brother Finger.
Here I am! Here I am!
How are you today?
Very well，thank you.
Run away. Run away.

Sister Finger，Sister Finger.
Here I am! Here I am!
How are you today?
Very well，thank you.
Run away. Run away.

Baby Finger，Baby Finger.
Here I am! Here I am!
How are you today?
Very well，thank you.
Run away. Run away.

词汇：father (Daddy)，mother (Mommy)，brother，sister，baby

歌曲 2

主题：Fruits and Adjectives

Apple

Apple round，apple red，
Apple juicy，apple sweet，
Apple，apple，I love you，
Apple sweet，I love to eat.

词汇：round，juicy，sweet

歌曲 3

主题：Farm Animals

Old MacDonald Had a Farm

Old MacDonald had a farm. EIEIO!
And on his farm he had a cow. EIEIO!
With a moo-moo here and a moo-moo there，
Here a moo! There a moo! Everywhere a moo—moo!
Old MacDonald had a farm. EIEIO!

Old MacDonald had a farm. EIEIO!
And on his farm he had a duck. EIEIO!
With a quack-quack here and a quack-quack there，
Here a quack! There a quack! Everywhere a quack-quack!
Old MacDonald had a farm. EIEIO!

Old MacDonald had a farm. EIEIO!
And on his farm he had a chick. EIEIO!
With a chick-chick here and a chick-chick there，
Here a chick! There a chick! Everywhere a chick-chick!
Old MacDonald had a farm. EIEIO!

Old MacDonald had a farm. EIEIO!
And on his farm he had a pig. EIEIO!
With an oink-oink here and an oink-oink there，
Here an oink! There an oink! Everywhere an oink-oink!

Old MacDonald had a farm. EIEIO!

词汇：cow，duck，chick，pig

歌曲 4

主题：字母 a 和 i 的读音

Two Little Black Birds

Two little black birds sitting on the hill,
One named Jack and the other named Jill.
Fly away Jack，fly away Jill.
Come back Jack，come back Jill.
Two little black birds sitting on the hill,
One named Jack and the other named Jill.

词汇：Jack，black，back，name，Jill，sit，little，hill

歌曲 5

主题：Body Parts

Head Shoulders Knees and Toes

Head and shoulders，knees and toes，knees and toes,
Head and shoulders，knees and toes，knees and toes,
Eyes and ears and mouth and nose,
Head and shoulders，knees and toes，knees and toes.

Head and shoulders，knees and toes，knees and toes,
Head and shoulders，knees and toes，knees and toes,
Eyes and ears and mouth and nose,
Head and shoulders，knees and toes，knees and toes.

词汇：head，shoulder，knee，toe，eye，ear，mouth，nose

歌曲 6

主题：Animals and Rooms in Homes

Animal House

There's a kangaroo in my kitchen.
There's a hippo in my hall.
There's a dinosaur in my dining-room,
A hundred metres tall!

My house is full of animals.
I don't know what to do.
I think I'm going crazy.
I'm living in a zoo!

There's a bison in my bathroom.
There's a beetle in my bed.
There's a tortoise in my toilet,
With a hamster on his head!
My house is full of animals.
I don't know what to do.
I think I'm going crazy.
I'm living in a zoo!

There's a gopher in my garden.
There's a tiger in my tree.
There's a lion in my living-room.
He's watching my TV!
My house is full of animals.
I don't know what to do.
I think I'm going crazy.
I'm living in a zoo!

My house is full of animals.
I don't know what to do.
I think I'm going crazy.
I'm living in a zoo!
I think I'm going crazy.
I'm living in a zoo!

词汇：kangaroo，hippo，dinosaur，bison，beetle，tortoise，hamster，gopher，tiger，lion，kitchen，hall，dining-room，bathroom，toilet，living-room

歌曲 7

主题： Days of the Week and Daily Activities

This Is the Way

This is the way we wash our clothes,
Wash our clothes, wash our clothes,
This is the way we wash our clothes,
So early Monday morning.

This is the way we iron our dress,
Iron our dress, iron our dress,
This is the way we iron our dress,
So early Tuesday morning.

This is the way we scrub the floor,
Scrub the floor, scrub the floor,
This is the way we scrub the floor,
So early Wednesday morning.

This is the way we mend our socks,
Mend our socks, mend our socks,
This is the way we mend our socks,
So early Thursday morning.

This is the way we sweep the house,
Sweep the house, sweep the house,
This is the way we sweep the house,
So early Friday morning.

This is the way we make our bread,
Make our bread, make our bread,
This is the way we make our bread,
So early Saturday morning.

This is the way we go to the farm,
Go to the farm, go to the farm,

This is the way we go to the farm,
So early Sunday morning.

词 汇：Sunday，Monday，Tuesday，Wednesday，Thursday，Friday，Saturday，wash our clothes，iron our dress，scrub the floor，mend our socks，sweep the house，make our bread，go to the farm

歌曲 8

主题： Daily Activities

Morning Round

I wake up every morning,
I get out of bed at six o'clock,
I wash my face and comb my hair,
Then，I put on my dress and shoes,
I have breakfast quickly,
Then，I always leave at seven o'clock,
I run to get the bus，and then,
I'm in my school right at eight,
I'm never late.

I wake up every morning,
I get out of bed at seven o'clock,
I wash my face and brush my teeth,
Then，I put on my clothes,
I eat my cereal quickly,
And I leave my house at half past seven,
I walk down to the subway，and
I arrive at eight o'clock a. m.
I'm never late.

I wake up every morning,
I get out of bed at six o'clock,
I take a shower and wash my hair,
Then，I put on my shirt and pants,
I eat an egg quickly,

Then, I take my books and leave at seven,
I see my friends and walk with them,
We always get to school at eight a. m.
We're never late.

She wakes up every morning,
She gets out of bed at six o'clock,
She washes her face and combs her hair,
Then, she puts on her dress and shoes,
She has breakfast quickly,
Then, she always leaves at seven o'clock,
She runs to get the bus, and then,
She's in her school right at eight,
She's never late.

He wakes up every morning,
He gets out of bed at seven o'clock,
He washes his face and brushes his teeth,
Then, he puts on his clothes,
He eats his cereal quickly,
And he leaves his house at half past seven,
He walks down to the subway, and
He arrives at eight o'clock a. m.
He's never late.

He wakes up every morning,
He gets out of bed at six o'clock,
He takes a shower and washes his hair,
Then, he puts on his shirt and pants,
He eats an egg quickly,
Then, he takes his books and leaves at seven,
He sees his friends and walks with them,
They always get to school at eight a. m.

They're never late.

词汇：wake up，get out of bed，wash my face，brush my teeth，comb my hair，wash my hair，take a shower，put on my clothes，have breakfast

歌曲 9

主题：一般过去时态

All on My Way to School

I went to school one morning，and walked like this，
Walked like this，walked like this.
I went to school one morning，and walked like this，
All on my way to school.

I saw a little robin，and he hopped like this，
Hopped like this，hopped like this，
I saw a little robin，and he hopped like this，
All on my way to school.

I saw a shiny river，and I splashed like this，
Splashed like this，splashed like this，
I saw a shiny river，and I splashed like this，
All on my way to school.

I saw a little horse，and he galloped like this，
Galloped like this，galloped like this，
I saw a little horse，and he galloped like this，
All on my way to school.

I saw a poor old lady，and she hobbled like this，
Hobbled like this，hobbled like this，
I saw a poor old lady，and she hobbled like this，
All on my way to school.

I saw a tall policeman，and he stood like this，
Stood like this，stood like this，

I saw a tall policeman, and he stood like this,
All on my way to school.

I heard school bell ringing, and I ran like this,
Ran like this, ran like this,
I heard school bell ringing, and I ran like this,
All on my way to school.
All on my way to school.

词汇：walk, hop, splash, gallop, hobble, stand, run

歌曲 10

主题：Occupation

Dream

If I were a cowboy, I'd ride on my horse.
If I were a pilot, I'd fly.
If I were a cop, I would be on the force.
If I were an actor, I'd cry.

If I were a singer, I'd sing you a tune.
If I were a tailor, I'd sew.
If I were a spaceman, I'd fly to the moon.
But wishing just won't make it so.

(Chorus)
If we want what we haven't got,
If we want to be what we're not,
We'll never be happy it seems,
We all want to live in our dream.

If you were a teacher, you'd teach me to write.
If you were an artist, you'd draw.
If you were a boxer, you'd win every fight.
If you were a carpenter, you'd saw.

If you were a banker，you'd have lots of money.
If you were a baker，you'd bake.
If you were a clown，you would be very funny.
If you were a gardener，you'd rake.
But wishing just won't make it so.

(Chorus)
If we want what we haven't got,
If we want to be what we're not,
We'll never be happy it seems,
We all want to live in our dream.

If I had an airplane，I'd fly you to France.
If I had a steamship，we'd sail.
If I owned a theatre，I'd ask you to dance.
If I fished，I'd bring you a whale.

If I climbed a mountain，I'd bring you a cloud.
If I were a rooster，I'd crow.
If I could tell jokes，you'd be laughing out loud.
But wishing just won't make it so.

(Chorus)
If we want what we haven't got,
If we want to be what we're not,
We'll never be happy it seems,
We all want to live in our dream.

词汇：cowboy，pilot，cop，actor，singer，tailor，spaceman，teacher，artist，boxer，carpenter，banker，baker，clown，gardener

第三节 诵读活动

诵读童谣（chant）是一项十分有益的教学活动。它可以用来训练学生的语音语调，增强学生的节奏感；它可以用于教授新的语言知识，加深学生对新学知识的印象；它也可以用于复习巩固所学知识，帮助学生记忆。即便是用来从一个教学活动过渡到下一个教学活动，童谣也深受学生喜欢。童谣还有一个相当重要的作用，那就是重构教材的文本，以满足不同层次学生的需求。当然，在文本重构的过程中，教师要注意以下几点：童谣的内容要富有情趣，语言要浅显易懂，音韵要自然和谐，关键词汇和句型要多反复几次。

童谣 1

主题：字母组合 ai，ay 的读音

Rain，Rain，Go Away

Rain，rain，go away.
Tom and Mary want to play.
Rain，rain，go away.
Come again another day.

词汇：rain，again，away，play，day

童谣 2

主题：字母 o 的读音

A Motor-car

Here comes a motor-car，
A motor-car，a motor-car，
Here comes a motor-car，
To go to London Town.

词汇：motor-car，London，town

童谣 3

主题：字母组合 ow 的读音

The Bus

The people on the bus go up and down，
Up and down，up and down.
The people on the bus go up and down，

All through the town.

词汇：down，town

童谣 4

主题：字母 o 的读音

Froggy-boggy

Froggy-boggy sat on a rock.

Froggy-boggy had a shock.

Froggy-boggy fell off the top.

Into the pond he fell with a plop.

词汇：Froggy-boggy，rock，shock，top，pond，plop

童谣 5

主题：Body parts

We Can Do Many Things

We can see with our eyes.

We can hear with our ears.

We can speak with our mouth.

We can smell with our nose.

We can taste with our tongue.

We can write with our hands.

We can walk with our legs.

We can do many things.

词汇：do，see，hear，speak，smell，taste，write，walk，thing，eye，ear，mouth，nose，tongue，hand，leg

童谣 6

主题：现在进行时态

Everything Is Moving Now

Everything is moving now.

Let me show you how.

My head is shaking，shaking.

My arms are waving，waving.

My legs are swinging，swinging.

词汇：move，shake，wave，swing

童谣7

主题：Animals

Animals

Dear elephant，dear elephant，
Why is your nose so long?
My mum's nose is very long.
So my nose is very long.

Dear giraffe，dear giraffe，
Why is your neck so long?
My mum's neck is long.
So my neck is long.

Dear fox，dear fox，
Why is your tail so long?
My mum's tail is long.
So my tail is long.

词汇：elephant，giraffe，fox

童谣8

主题：In the sky

What a Beautiful Day

What a beautiful day!
The sky is blue.
What a beautiful day!
The sun is shining.
What a beautiful night!
The moon is yellow.
What a beautiful night!
The stars are twinkling.

词汇：sky，sun，moon，star

童谣9

主题：Seasons

Seasons

Spring is warm with flower and song.
Summer is hot and the days are long.
Autumn is rich with fruit and grain.
Winter brings snow and the New Year again.

词汇：spring，warm，flower，song，summer，hot，day，long，autumn，rich，fruit，grain，winter，bring，snow，again

童谣 10

主题：Occupation

I Have Seen These People

Have you seen the postman，the postman，the postman?
Have you seen the postman who lives in the long lane?
I have seen the postman，the postman，the postman.
I have seen the postman who lives in the long lane.

Have you seen the milkman，the milkman，the milkman?
Have you seen the milkman who lives in the long lane?
I have seen the milkman，the milkman，the milkman.
I have seen the milkman who lives in the long lane.

Have you seen the policeman，the policeman，the policeman?
Have you seen the policeman who lives in the long lane?
I have seen the policeman，the policeman，the policeman.
I have seen the policeman who lives in the long lane.

Have you seen the spaceman，the spaceman，the spaceman?
Have you seen the spaceman who lives in the long lane?
I have seen the spaceman，the spaceman，the spaceman.
I have seen the spaceman who lives in the long lane.

词汇：postman，milkman，policeman，spaceman

第四节　值日生报告和自由演讲

报告 1

主题：School Subjects

Hello! I'm on duty today. In the morning we have Chinese, Maths, IT and English. In the afternoon we have Art and Music.

词汇：Chinese, Maths, English, Music, Art, PE, IT

报告 2

主题：Days and Dates

Good morning. I'm on duty today. Today is Monday. March 1st. we are all here. No one is absent.

词 汇：Sunday, Monday, Tuesday, Wednesday, Thursday, Friday, Saturday, January, February, March, April, May, June, July, August, September, October, November, December

报告 3

主题：Weather

Good morning! I'm on duty today. It's a fine day today. The sun is shining. It is not cold. It is warm.

词汇：fine, sunny, cloudy, windy, rainy, hot, warm, cool, cold

报告 4

主题：Holidays and Festivals

Hello! I'm on duty today. We are very happy. Today is Children's Day. We are going to celebrate our holiday this afternoon. We can sing. We can dance. We'll have a nice day!

词汇：New Year's Day, Spring Festival, Lantern Festival, Dragon Boat Festival, Mid-autumn Festival, Mother's Day, Father's Day, Children's Day, National Day, Thanksgiving Day, Halloween, Christmas

报告 5

主题：Announcement

Attention, please. I have an announcement to make. Next Friday we're going to visit the Great Wall. We'll set out at eight o'clock by school bus. Don't be late. The trip will take a day. So don't forget to bring your lunch.

词汇：announcement，Palace Museum，Summer Palace，Temple of Heaven，by bus，by metro，by train，by plane，on foot

演讲 1

主题：My family

Look at this photo. It's a photo of my family. There are five people in my family. My grandfather，my grandmother，my father，my mother and I. My grandparents are retired. My father is an engineer. My mother is a teacher. I am a pupil. I love my family.

词汇：photo，grandparent，engineer，retired

演讲 2

主题：My Class

My name is Liu Ying. I'm from Class 1，Grade 4，Xiangyang Primary School. There are forty pupils in our class. Twenty-two boys and eighteen girls. Wang Hai is the tallest in our class. Guo Xiang runs very fast. Ma Xiaoyan can sing very well. Zhao Lei can play the violin. We study together and play together. We are good friends.

词汇：tall，fast，run，sing，violin，together

演讲 3

主题：Firefighters

This is a photo of a fire station. These are firefighters. They wear uniforms. They train every day. They roll hoses and climb ladders. When there is a fire，they drive engines to get there. They save people and put out the fire. They are very brave.

词汇：fire station，firefighter，uniform，train，hose，ladder，engine

演讲 4

主题：My New Home

I have a new home. It is very big. The living room is big. It faces south. There is a lot of sunshine. The dining room is big. The kitchen is big. And the washroom is big. There are also two bedrooms，a study and a garden. My father likes the study very much because he can work there. My mother likes the kitchen very much because she likes cooking. I like the garden very much because I can play there. We are very happy.

词汇：face，south，sunshine，living room，dining room，kitchen，washroom，bedroom，study，garden

演讲5

主题： Love to grandparents

Chong Yang Festival is coming. This year it is on November 10th. I love my grandparents. I can show my love to them. I can give them cakes.

But love is more than a gift. Love can be a kiss or a hug, a smile or a song. When they are busy and tired, I can give them a cup of tea and a helping hand. I can set the table and sweep the floor. I think it is love.

When they are out, I can give them a phone call: "Are you fine? I miss you very much!" I think it is also love.

Love is more than a gift. Love is all.

词汇： festival, gift, kiss, hug, miss

第四章

呈现环节的设计

本章导读

学生做好了学习准备，该开始学习新的知识了。新的学习内容用什么方法来呈现，才能使学生有兴趣学习呢？哪些活动比较有效？呈现环节中要注意哪些问题？本章将介绍一些短小精悍、形式多样的活动，让学生从感知入手，愉快地进入学习过程。

呈现（presentation）环节也称为课堂导入，教师通过不同的方式呈现新的学习内容，引导学生进入学习新知识的积极状态。在课堂教学各环节中，课堂导入是课堂教学的前奏。教育家董政枢曾说："好的开头，有如春色初展，鲜花含露，叫人钟情。"英语谚语也说："A good beginning is half the battle."（好的开端是成功的一半）一节课的导入恰到好处，便能在开课伊始就牢牢吸引学生的注意力，使其产生浓厚的兴趣和强烈的求知欲，在心理和知识上做好学习的准备，迅速进入良好的学习状态，从而为整堂课各项教学活动的顺利展开奠定良好的基础。因此，对于一节课的成功，课堂导入起着至关重要的作用。

导之有法，导无定法。导入没有固定的模式，教师可以根据不同的教学对象、教学目标、教学要求、教学内容，设计不同的导入方法。在这一环节的设计中，教师要注意以下几点：

1. 紧扣教学目标和内容

呈现（presentation）、操练（practice）、应用（production）是英语课堂教学过程中的三个重要环节。呈现的内容就是本课时的教学内容，所以它必须紧扣教学目标，与学生要学习的内容一致。

2. 切合学生的学习实际

教材的内容是预定的，但呈现的方法是多样的。教师要根据学生学习的实际情况，选用难易度适中的呈现方法，使学生在自然的状态中进入学习过程。

3. 把握课堂教学的节奏

呈现只是导入新授内容的方式，所以这个环节所用的时间不能过长，一般控制在10分钟之内。课堂教学时间主要用于操练环节和应用环节，主要目的是使学生掌握所学内容，完成学习目标。

第一节　以旧带新呈现

孔子曰："温故而知新。"回顾旧知识是导入新知识常用的方法之一。学习语言知识，培养学生能力，要周而复始，循序渐进。教材提供了一种螺旋式上升、前后有机衔接的知识体系，要求教师在导入新知识时，根据知识之间的逻辑关系，找准新旧知识的连接点，从学生已知的词汇、句型出发，引出新的知识点，激发学生的求知欲，创设传授新知识的最佳契机。

案例1

主题：Fruits

教学目标：能询问复数物品的名称和重量

教学内容：

句型：What are these?

What are those?

How many kilos?

呈现方法：

教师先出示bananas，grapes，pineapples，watermelons的图片，要求学生拼读这些单词，然后提问What are these，以已知词汇带出新授句型。

案例2

主题：Numbers

教学目标：学会数字6～10

教学内容：

词汇：six，seven，eight，nine，ten

呈现方法：

教师出示一张五岁男孩和一张六岁女孩的图画，画中都有生日蛋糕，上面各插着五支和六支蜡烛。先介绍五岁的男孩，复习数字1～5。

This is Tom. How old is he? Let's count the candles. One，two，three，four，five. Five candles. He is five.

然后介绍六岁的女孩，导入数字6。

This is Linda. How old is she? Let's count the candles. One, two, three, four, five, six. Six candles. She is six.

案例 3

主题： Making a Telephone Call

教学目标： 掌握打电话的基本表达方式

教学内容：

句型：May I speak to…?

Who is speaking?

This is…speaking.

Hold the line, please.

Can I take a message?

呈现方法：

从复习数字开始。要求学生听录音，记录座机号、手机号、QQ 号等等。

Phone number 010-58734209

Mobile phone number 18935724608

QQ number 14339720586

然后导入主题，教授打电话的基本表达方式。

案例 4

主题： 名词性物主代词

教学目标： 掌握名词性物主代词的用法

教学内容：

词汇：mine, yours, his, hers

句型：Whose…?

呈现方法：

教师通过提问复习形容词性物主代词。

Whose book is this?

Is this your school bag?

Is this his pen?

Is this her pencil-box?

然后导入名词性物主代词。

This is my book.

The book is mine.

This is your school bag.

This school bag is yours.

This is his pen.

This pen is his.

This is her pencil-box.

This pencil-box is hers.

案例 5

主题： Home Life

教学目标： 掌握现在进行时态

教学内容：

Home Life

I'm Cindy. I'm in the living room. I'm doing my homework. My father and my mother are in the kitchen. My mother is cooking. My father is helping her.

呈现方法：

先复习句型 Where is…? Where are…? 和词汇 living room，bedroom，washroom，kitchen。

然后呈现现在进行时态 Cindy is in the living room. She is doing her homework. Her father and mother are in the kitchen. Her mother is cooking. Her father is helping her mother.

第二节　直观感知呈现

心理学研究证明：识别一件物品，通过语言描述需要 2.8 秒，观看线条图画需要 1.5 秒，观看黑白照片需要 1.2 秒，观看彩色照片需要 0.9 秒，直接观看原物体只需要 0.4 秒。因此，在新授词汇的导入环节运用直观手段进行教学，形象鲜明生动，令人印象深刻。

案例 1

主题： Signs

教学目标： 能正确说出所学标识的含义

教学内容：

句型：What does this sign say? It says….

What does this sign mean? It means….

What does this sign tell us? It tells us….

呈现方法：

直接向学生出示本课要学的标识，如字母 P，I；单词 entrance，exit，stop，free wifi

或图标 restaurant，toilet，telephone，taxi，no smoking，no littering，no swimming，no fishing，告诉学生 These are signs。

然后拼读生词 sign，揭示本课话题。

教师可以用陈述句 This sign says…. This sign means…. This sign tells us…. 依次介绍这些标识，导入新知识。

案例 2

主题：Our Classroom Building

教学目标：能介绍教学楼中不同用途的教室

教学内容：

词汇：classroom，music room，art room，computer room，science room，dancing room，washroom，library，gym，on the first floor，on the second floor

句型：There is…. There are….

呈现方法：

教师用简笔画画出一栋两层的教学楼，标上各种用途教室的英语名称，以此呈现新授内容。

This is our classroom building. It has two floors. On the first floor there are many classrooms. There is also a gym. It is very big. On the second floor there is a music room，an art room，a computer room，a dancing room，a library. The washrooms are at the end of each floor.

案例 3

主题：Ability

教学目标：表达自己能做的事

教学内容：

词汇：read，write，sing，dance，draw

句型：I can….

呈现方法：

教师用肢体语言演示上述 5 个动作，用直观的方式呈现新授内容。

案例 4

主题：Colours

教学目标：能表达颜色

教学内容：

词汇：red，orange，yellow，green，blue，purple，white，black，pink，grey

句型：What colour is it? It is….

呈现方法 1：

出示一幅彩虹的图画，直接指着彩虹中不同的颜色呈现新授内容。

呈现方法 2：

准备一些一次性塑料杯、颜料和画笔，在水杯中放入颜料以呈现颜色，或用两种颜色相加调出第三种颜色。

red + white = pink

yellow + blue = green

white + black = grey

red + yellow = orange

blue + red = purple

red + green = black

案例 5

主题： Plants

教学目标： 能简单描述植物

教学内容：

词汇：root，stem，trunk，branch，leaf，flower

句型：It has….

They have….

呈现方法：

制作课件，用动画展示植物生长过程，然后依次呈现词汇与句型。

Look at the plant. It has roots. It has leaves. The leaves are green. It grows and grows. Now it has a stem. It has a flower. The flower is red. It is beautiful.

These are trees. They are big and tall. They have a trunk. They have branches. They have many leaves. Some trees have flowers. Some don't. They make the world beautiful.

第三节　视听活动呈现

案例 1

主题： Weather

教学目标： 能简单谈论天气

教学内容：

词汇：sunny，cloudy，rainy，windy，snowy

句型：How's the weather today? It's….

呈现方法：

播放视频，逐一呈现 sunny，cloudy，rainy，windy，snowy 的气象并教授这些单词。

案例 2

主题： Musical Instruments

教学目标： 学会乐器名称 piano，violin，triangle，drum

教学内容：

词汇：piano，violin，triangle，drum

句型：I can play….

呈现方法：

播放视频和音频，逐一呈现乐器 piano，violin，triangle，drum 和这些乐器的音色并教授这些单词。

案例 3

主题： Linda's Week

教学目标： 能用频度副词 always，usually，often，sometimes，never 描述他人一周的生活

教学内容：

词汇：always，usually，often，sometimes，never

呈现方法 1：

播放一段 Linda 自述一周生活的视频，然后教师用提问的方式与学生谈论 Linda 一周的生活，导入新授内容。

What does Linda do at school?

What does Linda do after school?

What does Linda do at weekends?

呈现方法 2：

先发给学生一份表格，然后播放一段 Linda 自述一周生活的录音，让学生整体感知新授内容，边听边在表格上打"√"。

	at school	after school	at weekends
play ball games			
play computer games			
go to the children's palace			
go to the club			

续前表

	at school	after school	at weekends
go to the school library			
do projects			
do homework			
have many lessons			

然后根据统计的频度讲解这些副词的用法。

案例 4

主题： Means of Transportation

教学目的： 掌握一些表示交通工具的词汇

教学内容：

词汇：bicycle，motor-car，car，bus，tram，metro，ship，plane

句型：I go to… by….

呈现方法：

制作课件，用动画呈现不同的交通工具，并配上音响效果，然后教授词汇和句型。

案例 5

主题： Children's Day

教学目的： 掌握现在进行时

教学内容：

Children's Day

Good morning! My name is Li Liang. I'm from Xinhua Primary School. Today is Children's Day. The children are very happy.

Now I'm on the playground. Look, the children are doing sports. Some are running. Some are jumping. They are having a match!

Now I'm in the garden. Look, the children are playing games. Some are playing hide-and-seek. Some are playing duck-duck-goose. They are having fun.

Now I'm in the music room. Look, the children are having a party. Some are singing. Some are dancing. They are having a good time.

What a happy Children's Day. This is Li Liang at Xinhua Primary School.

呈现方法：

预先制作好录像。把教学内容用画面呈现出来。让学生边看录像，边听小记者的报道。

案例 6

主题： The Giant's Garden

教学目标：理解故事，掌握关键词汇与句型，并能复述故事。

教学内容：

The Giant's Garden

A giant lives in a castle. In the castle there is a beautiful garden. Children like to play in his garden. They run. They jump. They fly kites. They climb trees. They are very happy. But the giant is not happy. He is angry. He shouts, "Get out!" The children are afraid and run away. The giant builds a tall wall around the garden and puts up a sign "Keep out" on the wall. Now the children cannot play in his garden.

Miss Spring comes. She brings beautiful flowers and birds. She sees the sign. So she does not go there. The giant looks at his garden. There is no flower. There is no bird. There is only snow. It is still winter in his garden. He feels very cold and sad.

One morning, the giant hears birds singing. He smells flowers. He looks out of the window. He sees many children in his garden. They come into the garden through a hole in the wall. They bring Miss Spring into his garden. The giant is happy. He breaks down the wall and lets the children play in his garden. The garden is beautiful. And it is full of joy.

呈现方法：

播放故事的视频，让学生先观看整个故事，然后分段教授故事。

第四节 组织游戏呈现

孔子曰："知之者不如好之者，好之者不如乐之者。"根据不同的教学内容，采用不同的游戏来呈现新授内容，不仅能为新授内容做好铺垫，还能有效激发学生的学习兴趣。

案例 1

主题：On the Farm

教学目标：能简单介绍农场动物

教学内容：

词汇：pig，horse，cow，sheep，chick，duck

句型：This is….

呈现方法 1：

教师播放预录的农场动物的叫声，让学生猜那是什么动物发出的叫声，然后出示这个动物的图像，介绍这个动物。

呈现方法2：

教师用幻灯片显示预制的农场动物的部分身体，让学生猜那是什么动物，然后出示这个动物的完整图像，介绍这个动物。

呈现方法3：

教师用简单的英语描述某一农场动物，让学生猜那是什么动物。学生猜中后教师出示这个动物的图像，介绍这个动物。

案例2

主题： Food and Drinks

教学目标： 掌握不可数名词数量的表达方式

教学内容：

词组：a box of milk，a bottle of wine，a can of meat，a bag of rice

呈现方法：

教师和学生一起讨论，把需要购买的物品写在购物单上，然后呈现表达不可数名词数量的词组。

案例3

主题： Time

教学目标： 能表达现在时刻

教学内容：

词汇：past，to

句型：What's the time? It's….

What time is it? It's….

呈现方法：

先做游戏复习数字11～20。

然后导入时间的表达方式。

案例4

主题： Sports

教学目标： 能表达自己喜欢的球类活动

教学内容：

词组：play football，play ping-pong，play basketball，play badminton

句型：I like playing….

呈现方法：

教师准备上述球类活动的图片，给一名学生看，并请他用肢体语言表现出来，让其他学生猜这是什么球类活动，以此方法呈现新授内容。

案例 5

主题：一般过去时态

教学目的：掌握 Be 动词的过去形式和用法

教学内容：

词汇：was，were（Be 动词的过去形式）

呈现方法：

播放一组班上某一学生小时候的照片，然后请学生猜这是谁。

Look at these pictures. These are the pictures of your classmate. In the first picture he was one month old. In the second picture he was one year old. In the third picture he was three years old. In the fourth picture he was with his father and mother. In the fifth picture he was in the kindergarten. Who is he? Can you guess?

以此方法呈现 Be 动词的过去形式和用法。

第五节　创设情境呈现

利用与多媒体创设及教材所呈现的材料相匹配的真实环境，使学生身临其境地学习新知识，是英语教师常用的有效方法。

案例 1

主题：Food and Drinks

教学目标：能简单表达自己的需求

教学内容：

词汇：hotdog，hamburger，pizza，sandwich

句型：I want….

呈现方法：

用多媒体创设出快餐店的情境，然后用幻灯片显示快餐店的价目表，逐一教授生词。

案例 2

主题：Seeing the Doctor

教学目标：学习就医的对话，掌握基本表达方式

教学内容：

Seeing the Doctor

Doctor：What's wrong with you?

Patient：I don't feel well. I have a headache.

Doctor：Let me have a look at you. Open your mouth. Say "Ah".

Patient：Ah.

Doctor：Now take a deep breath. Good. You have a flu. Take some medicine. Drink plenty of water. You'll soon be better.

Patient：Thank you，Doctor.

呈现方法：

教师穿上白大褂，准备一些简单的用具，扮演医生，营造就医的氛围，然后开始教授对话。

案例 3

主题：Asking the Way

教学目标：掌握问路的基本表达方式

教学内容：

句型：Excuse me. Where is…?

How can I get to…? You can….

呈现方法：

按教学内容重新摆放教室里的桌椅，桌上放置目的地和公交站牌，然后开始教学活动。

案例 4

主题：The Insect Museum

教学目标：学习、理解所学内容，并能简单介绍昆虫博物馆

教学内容：

The Insect Museum

This is the insect museum. In the insect museum there are many kinds of insect specimens. They are butterflies，ladybirds，mantises，dragonflies and so on. We can see the most beautiful butterfly in the world. Its wings can change colours. We can watch movies about the lifecycle of some insects. We can also make insect specimens by ourselves. We can learn a lot in the insect museum.

呈现方法：

利用视频播放昆虫馆的展品，让学生有身临其境的感受，边参观边学习。

案例 5

主题： Make a Jack-o'-lantern

教学目标： 了解西方节日，制作一盏鬼脸灯

教学内容：

Make a Jack-o'-lantern

First, take a big orange. Second, cut a face, two eyes and a big mouth. Third, cut the top. Don't throw it away. Fourth, take out the inside. Fifth, put a small candle inside the orange and light it. Now, you have a Jack-o'-lantern for Halloween!

呈现方法：

在教室里布置万圣节前夜的环境，为节日的到来营造气氛。

教师先展示自己的鬼脸灯，然后发给每个小组一个大橙子，让学生制作鬼脸灯。

第六节　问答呈现

在课堂教学的呈现环节，巧妙运用问答对话，能激活学生的思维，调动学生的学习兴趣，为呈现新的语言知识做自然的铺垫。

案例 1

主题： Mother's Day

教学目标： 谈论母亲节能为母亲做的事

教学内容：

词组：write a letter, make a carnation, give Mum a hug and a kiss, make a cup of tea for Mum

呈现方法：

教师可以先提问 What day is today，也可以先介绍 Mother's Day，然后提问 What can we do for Mum，接着让学生充分发表意见，最后依次学习本课的教学内容。

案例 2

主题： Seasons and Clothes

教学目标： 能表达不同的季节以及适宜在不同季节穿的衣服

教学内容：

It is spring. It is nice and warm. I wear my shirt and sweater.

It is summer. It is sunny and hot. I wear my T-shirt and shorts.

It is autumn. It is windy and cool. I wear my coat and trousers.

It is winter. It is snowy and cold. I wear my scarf and gloves.

呈现方法：

教师在出示相关图片后通过提问导入新授内容：

Do you like spring?

How is the weather in spring?

What clothes do you wear in spring?

案例 3

主题： Children's Day

教学目标： 能介绍不同国家的儿童节

教学内容：

Children's Day

In China, Children's Day is on June 1st.

In the UK, Children's Day is on July 14th.

In Singapore, Children's Day is on October 1st.

In Thailand, Children's Day is on January 2nd.

In Japan, there are two Children's Days. The Children's Day for girls is on March 3rd. The Children's Day for boys is on May 5th.

呈现方法：

教师出示一本月历，然后提问导入主题：

What day is January 1st?

What day is May 1st?

What day is June 1st?

案例 4

主题： Spring Festival

教学目标： 能简单介绍春节的习俗

教学内容：

Spring Festival

Spring Festival usually comes in January or February. The weather is cold and dry. People eat dumplings and spring rolls. They buy new clothes and traditional food. On New Year's Eve, families have a big dinner together. After dinner they watch Spring Festival Gala and colourful fireworks. Children get money in red envelopes. During Spring Festival, people visit their relatives and friends. They say Happy New Year to each other. They are happy to be together.

呈现方法：

教师出示有关春节习俗的图片，然后通过提问导入新授内容：

Which festival do you like best?

What do you want to say?

What do you want to eat?

What do you want to buy?

案例 5

主题： A Famous Person

教学目标： 能介绍人物

教学内容：

Thomas Edison

Thomas Edison was a great inventor. He was born in 1847. Even when he was very young, he showed great interest in science. He was at school for only a few months, but he became the greatest inventor in the 20th century. He invented the light bulb, the phonograph and many other things. All his inventions are very useful in our lives. Thomas Edison died in 1931 at the age of 84.

呈现方法：

教师把写有这位发明家名字的卡片给一位学生看，其他学生通过提问猜这位发明家是谁。卡片持有者只能用“yes”或“no”来回答，在特殊情况下可给予适当提示。学生猜中后开始学习具体内容。

第七节　歌曲呈现

英语歌曲具有优美动听的旋律和轻松活泼的节奏。选用与新授内容关系密切的歌曲来进行课堂导入，不仅能提高学生的学习兴趣，而且可以活跃气氛，创造语言环境。采用听、唱英语歌曲的教学手段，可以让学生在轻松愉快的氛围中掌握新知识，体验学习英语的快乐。

案例 1

主题： Weather

教学目标： 能简单谈论天气

教学内容：

词汇：sunny，cloudy，rainy，windy，snowy

句型：How's the weather today? It's….

呈现方法：

教师播放 How's the Weather 这首歌，如果学生已经学过这首歌，也可以让他们一起唱，然后学习句型和词汇。

How's the Weather

How's the weather?
How's the weather?
How's the weather today?
Is it sunny?
Is it rainy?
Is it cloudy?
Is it snowy?
How's the weather today?

Let's look outside.
How's the weather?
Is it sunny today?
Let's look outside.
How's the weather?
Is it rainy today?
Let's look outside.
How's the weather?
Is it cloudy today?
Let's look outside.
Is it snowy today?

案例 2

主题： In the Sky

教学目标： 能简单描述天体及天体现象

教学内容：

词汇：sky，sun，moon，star，shine，twinkle

句型：Look at….

呈现方法：

教师播放 Twinkle，Twinkle，Little Star 这首歌，如果学生已经学过这首歌，也可以让他们一起唱，然后学习句型和词汇。

Twinkle，Twinkle，Little Star

Twinkle，twinkle，little star，
How I wonder what you are，
Up above the world so high，
Like a diamond in the sky.

案例 3

主题：现在进行时态

教学目标：能表达现在正在做的动作

教学内容：

词汇：walk，hop，run，jump，swing，swim

呈现方法：

教师播放 Walking，Walking 这首歌，同时用肢体语言帮助学生理解。如果学生已经学过这首歌，可以让他们边唱边做动作，然后拼读新授单词。

Walking，Walking

Walking，walking.
Walking，walking.
Hop，hop，hop.
Hop，hop，hop.
Running，running，running.
Running，running，running.
Now let's stop.
Now let's stop.

Walking，walking.
Walking，walking.
Hop，hop，hop.
Hop，hop，hop.

Running, running, running.
Running, running, running.
Now let's stop.
Now let's stop.

Tiptoe, tiptoe.
Tiptoe, tiptoe.
Jump, jump.
Jump, jump.
Swing, swing, swing.
Swing, swing, swing.
Now let's sleep.
Now let's sleep.

Wake up!
It's time to go!
Are you ready to go fast?
Okay!

Walking, walking.
Walking, walking.
Hop, hop, hop.
Hop, hop, hop.
Running, running, running.
Running, running, running.
Now let's stop.
Now let's stop.

Walking, walking.
Walking, walking.
Hop, hop, hop.
Hop, hop, hop.
Running, running, running.

Running，running，running.

Now let's stop.

Now let's stop.

Whew!

案例 4

主题： Seasons and Clothes

教学目标： 掌握 4 个表示服饰的词汇，并能运用 Put on…等句型

教学内容：

词汇：shoe，jacket，scarf，hat

句型：Put on….

　　　Take off….

呈现方法：

教师播放 Put on Your Shoes 这首歌，如果学生已经学过这首歌，也可以让他们一起唱，然后学习句型和词汇。

Put on Your Shoes

Put on your shoes，your shoes，your shoes.

Put on your shoes，your shoes，your shoes.

Put on your shoes.

Let's go outside.

Hurry up. Hurry up. Hurry，hurry up!

Put on your jacket，your jacket，your jacket.

Put on your jacket，your jacket，your jacket.

Put on your jacket.

Let's go outside.

Hurry up. Hurry up. Hurry，hurry up!

Put on your scarf，your scarf，your scarf.

Put on your scarf，your scarf，your scarf.

Put on your scarf.

Let's go outside.

Hurry up. Hurry up. Hurry，hurry up!

Put on your hat，your hat，your hat.
Put on your hat，your hat，your hat.
Put on your hat.
Let's go outside.
Hurry up. Hurry up. Hurry，hurry up!

Put on your shoes.
Your jacket.
Your scarf.
Your hat.
Hurry up. Hurry up. Hurry，hurry up!

案例 5

主题：Animals in the Zoo

教学目标：能简单介绍动物园里的动物

教学内容：

词汇：elephant，lion，tiger，bear，panda，monkey

句型：Do you like…？Yes，I do. /No，I don't.

呈现方法：

教师播放 Let's Go to the Zoo 这首歌，如果学生已经学过这首歌，也可以让他们一起唱，然后学习句型和词汇。

Let's Go to the Zoo

Stomp like elephants!
Let's go to the zoo
And stomp like the elephants do.
Let's go to the zoo
And stomp like the elephants do.

Jump like kangaroos.
Let's go to the zoo
And jump like the kangaroos do.

Let's go to the zoo
And jump like the kangaroos do.

Swing like monkeys.
Let's go to the zoo
And Swing like monkeys do.
Let's go to the zoo
And Swing like monkeys do.

Waddle like penguins.
Let's go to the zoo
And waddle like penguins do.
Let's go to the zoo
And waddle like penguins do.

Slither like snakes.
Let's go to the zoo
And slither like the snakes do.
Let's go to the zoo
And slither like the snakes do.

Swim like polar bears.
Let's go to the zoo
And swim like polar bears do.
Let's go to the zoo
And swim like polar bears do.

Let's go to the zoo
And dance like the animals do.
Let's go to the zoo
And dance like the animals do.

案例 6

主题： 一般过去时态

教学目的： 掌握Be动词的过去形式和用法

教学内容：

词汇：was，were（Be动词的过去形式）

呈现方法：

教师请学生一起唱Bingo，利用歌词呈现be动词的过去形式和用法。

Bingo

There was a farmer had a dog.
And Bingo was his name. Oh!
B-I-N-G-O，B-I-N-G-O，B-I-N-G-O.
And Bingo was his name. Oh!

There was a farmer had a dog.
And Bingo was his name. Oh!
(Clap) -I-N-G-O，(Clap) -I-N-G-O，(Clap) -I-N-G-O.
And Bingo was his name. Oh!

There was a farmer had a dog.
And Bingo was his name. Oh!
(Clap-Clap) -N-G-O，(Clap-Clap) -N-G-O，(Clap-Clap) -N-G-O.
And Bingo was his name. Oh!

There was a farmer had a dog.
And Bingo was his name. Oh!
(Clap-Clap-Clap) -G-O，(Clap-Clap-Clap) -G-O，(Clap-Clap-Clap) -G-O.
And Bingo was his name. Oh!

There was a farmer had a dog.
And Bingo was his name. Oh!
(Clap-Clap-Clap-Clap) -O，(Clap-Clap-Clap-Clap) -O，(Clap-Clap-Clap-Clap) -O.
And Bingo was his name. Oh!

There was a farmer had a dog.

And Bingo was his name. Oh!
(Clap-Clap-Clap-Clap-Clap),
(Clap-Clap-Clap-Clap-Clap),
(Clap-Clap-Clap-Clap-Clap),
And Bingo was his name. Oh!

There was a farmer had a dog.
And Bingo was his name. Oh!
B-I-N-G-O, B-I-N-G-O, B-I-N-G-O.
And Bingo was his name. Oh!

第八节 童谣呈现

童谣简单易记、朗朗上口，配上简单的动作或与之相配的韵律节奏，不仅能活跃气氛，而且能培养学生的语感。当然，童谣的选择和编排应该以本节课的教学目标为出发点，要有导向性。

案例 1

主题： Numbers

教学目标： 掌握数字 1～10

教学内容：

词汇：one，two，three，four，five，six，seven，eight，nine，ten

呈现方法：

教师播放童谣 Buckle My Shoe，要求学生注意童谣中的数字。如果学生已经学过这首童谣，也可以让他们一起吟诵，然后拼读数字。

Buckle My Shoe

One, two,
Buckle my shoe;
Three, four,
Open the door;
Five, six,

Pick up sticks;
Seven, eight,
Lay them straight;
Nine, ten,
A big, fat hen.

案例2

主题： Shapes

教学目标： 能简单谈论形状

教学内容：

词汇：circle, square, triangle, star, rectangle

句型：What shape is it? It is a….

呈现方法：

教师播放童谣Make a Circle，可以让学生边听边做动作，然后一起吟诵，并学习词汇与句型。

Make a Circle

Make a circle, big, big, big.
Small, small, small.
Big, big, big.
Make a circle small, small, small.
Hello, hello, hello.

Make a circle, round and round.
Round and round.
Round and round.
Make a circle, round and round.
Hello, hello, hello.

Make a circle, up, up, up.
Down, down, down.
Up, up, up.
Make a circle, down, down, down.
Now sit down.

案例3

主题：Food

教学目标：能表达自己喜欢的食品

教学内容：

词汇：apple，orange，banana，peach，pear

句型：I like….

呈现方法：

教师播放童谣 Are You Hungry，也可以让学生一起吟诵，然后学习词汇与句型。

Are You Hungry

Are you hungry?
Yes，I am.
Me，too.
Let's eat!

Are you hungry?
Yes，I am.
Are you hungry?
Yes，I am.
Mmmmm，a banana!
Yum，yum，yum，yum，yum，yum，yum，yum，yum.

Are you hungry?
Yes，I am.
Are you hungry?
Yes，I am.
Mmmmm，watermelon!
Yum，yum，yum，yum，yum，yum，yum，yum，yum.

Are you hungry?
Yes，I am.
Are you hungry?
Yes，I am.

Mmmmm，French fries!
Yum，yum，yum，yum，yum，yum，yum，yum，yum.

Are you hungry?
Yes，I am.
Are you hungry?
Yes，I am.
Mmmmm，spaghetti!
Yum，yum，yum，yum，yum，yum，yum，yum，yum.

Are you hungry?
Yes，I am.
Are you hungry?
Yes，I am.
Mmmmm，ice cream!
Yum，yum，yum，yum，yum，yum，yum，yum，yum.

I'm full.

案例 4

主题：介词

教学目标：掌握介词 in 和 on 的基本用法

教学内容：

介词：in，on

句型：Pick up…. Put….

呈现方法：

教师播放童谣 Clean up。如果学生学过，可以让他们一起吟诵，然后学习词汇与句型。

Clean up

Clean up，clean up.
Everybody，let's clean up.
Clean up，clean up.
Put your things away.
(Four times)

Clean up! Clean up! Clean up!
Put your things away.
Pick up your toys.
Pick up your books.
Pick up your shoes.
Put your things away.

Clean up, clean up.
Everybody, let's clean up.
Clean up, clean up.
Put your things away.
(Two times)

案例5

主题: Toys

教学目标: 能表达自己想要的玩具

教学内容:

词汇:train, doll, rocket, skateboard

句型:I want….

呈现方法:

教师播放童谣What Do You Want for Christmas,也可以让学生边听童谣边看这些圣诞礼物,然后学习词汇与句型。

What Do You Want for Christmas

What do you want for Christmas? Christmas? Christmas?
What do you want for Christmas?
Santa's on his way.
I want a train.
I want a train.
I want a great big train.
A train?
A train.

What do you want for Christmas? Christmas? Christmas?

What do you want for Christmas?

Santa's on his way.

I want a rocket.

I want a rocket.

I want a great big rocket.

A rocket?

A rocket.

Prepare for lift off. Five, four, three, two, one. Lift off!

What do you want for Christmas? Christmas? Christmas?

What do you want for Christmas?

Santa's on his way.

I want a robot.

I want a robot.

I want a great big robot.

A robot?

A robot.

What do you want for Christmas? Christmas? Christmas?

What do you want for Christmas?

Santa's on his way.

I want a teddy bear.

I want a teddy bear.

I want a great big teddy bear.

A teddy bear?

A teddy bear.

Right leg. Left leg. Right arm. Left arm. Oh no!

What do you want for Christmas? Christmas? Christmas?

What do you want for Christmas?

Santa's on his way.

Santa's on his way!

第五章

操练环节的设计

本章导读

新的知识讲完了，该进行操练了。操练环节非常重要，因为学生只有通过操练活动，才能够使信息内化为认知结构的一部分，才算学会了新知识。本章将介绍如何设计各种各样的活动使学生巩固所学的新知识，使操练环节真正具有实效性。

第一节　听的操练

听是指小学生吸收和理解语言材料所载信息的能力，是一种有目的的交际行为，是一种积极的心理语言活动过程，是一种主动的、隐性的技能。

据美国外语教学专家的统计，在听说读写活动中，听占实际时间的45%，说占30%，读占16%，写占9%。可见，听在人类交际活动中起着十分重要的作用。因此，在听的操练环节，教师要紧紧围绕教学目标创设良好的听的语境；要精心选择材料，以多种形式进行有效的听的训练；要充分调动非智力因素，促进听的效果，在听的基础上提高学生的英语综合运用能力。

一、听的形式

在操练环节，教师可采用静听、听音模仿与重复、听音示意、听与写结合、听与说结合等形式来进行操练。

（一）静听

1. 听辨练习

在静听环节，教师可以让学生进行听辨练习。学生在基本掌握单词发音之后，被要求列出与所学单词相似的曾经学过的单词。

案例 1

听教师读一组音素或单词，学生指出其元音发音是否相同。

[uː] —— [u] （×）

[uː] —— [uː] （√）

[v] —— [w] （×）

[tuː] —— [tuː] （√）

[miːt] — [miːt] （√）

[bæd] —— [bed] （×）

bag——big （×）

game——man （×）

案例 2

听教师读一组单词，学生指出单词中的不同音素。

[tuː] —— [tu] （元音不同；[uː] —— [u]）

[siːt] —— [miːt] （辅音不同；[s] —— [m]）

案例 3

让学生听所学的新词，并举出一定数量的与所学新词元音相同的单词。

bar

car，pass，hard，glass，father

cake

game，name

bag

hat，man，cat

cow

how，now

案例 4

让学生听所学的新词，并指出下列单词画线部分的发音是否与新词相同。

classr<u>oo</u>m

cook　(×)

afternoon　(√)

案例 5

听老师念 A 栏中的单词，然后从 B 栏中选出与 A 栏中元音相同的单词，分别填在相应单词后边的括号内。

A		B
cake	(same)	red
bike	(Mike)	girl
bed	(red)	same
worker	(girl)	Mike

案例 6

听音编绕口令

在学了 jeep 一词后，教师可扩充相关发音规律的单词，让学生静听几遍后试着编绕口令。

在学了交通工具 bike 等单词后，除了操练 bike 中的元音字母/ai/的发音外，教师还可以补充一些有着相同发音规律的单词，让学生在静听的基础上编绕口令。

在静听中辨别单词的相同与不同，能使学生进一步分清所学单词的发音，为学生读准单词做了对比方面的加强。

2. 听小短文

在学习完新知识后，教师还可选择一篇与所学知识相关的小短文让学生静听，方式可以是亲自朗读或听录音，然后让学生用所学的单词、句型来回答问题。

案例 1

Oxford English Book 4A（上海版）

Module 1 Unit 3 Feelings

教材文本：

Sam and Ginger

Kitty & Ben：Hi，Peter.

Peter：Hi，Kitty. Hi，Ben. Come in，please.

Peter：Sit down，please.

Kitty：Thank you.

Ben：Sorry. Sam is thirsty.

Peter：But it's Ginger's water.

Ben：Thanks，Peter. Sam is happy now.

Peter：Are you thirsty too，Ginger? Here's some water for you.

Ben：They don't like each other.

教师根据教材文本编写了一段新文本让学生静听录音：

Animals Have Feelings

Animals have feelings，just like you and me.

Let's take dog as an example.

When a dog is happy，it may wag its tail.

When a dog is sick，it may lie on the ground.

When a dog is sad，it may hide from you.

When a dog is angry，it may pee in your shoes.

For animals have feelings，we must be nice to them.

教师通过该文本不断操练重点句型 How does he/she feel? He's…/She's…/When…，it may…同时在操练中教授了动词 wag，hide，lie，pee 等。由于教师提供的新文本有孩子们丰富的生活经验和积极的情感态度做支撑，因此，操练变得真实而有效。

（二）听音模仿与重复

听音模仿与重复是提高学生表达能力的重要途径，在听的操练环节中不可忽视，因为它是使学生具有良好语音、语调的基础。小学生最主要的模仿对象，一个是教师，一个是录音。

1. 模仿教师读单词是模仿录音读单词的前提

在听的操练环节中，教师会给学生提供一些新的语言材料，教授新单词在所难免。此时，教师一定要注意让学生看自己的口型，从一开始就培养学生听音模仿单个音素、音节。操练要从单音节词、双音节词到多音节词，注重单词重音、辅音连缀、浊化、失去爆破及句子语调等。操练应遵循先听再模仿的顺序，教师可重复两到三遍。在呈现单词时，先呈现单词的义，然后让学生听发音，最后给出词形。音、义结合，让学生更好地掌握每个单词。具体而言，操练有如下步骤：

(1) 让学生认真倾听教师的发音，通过出示实物或图片让学生理解单词的词义。如 bread，给学生一个整体感知。

(2) 跟读模仿，如果是多音节词，教师一定要按发音分开带读，让学生听清每个音节的发音，如 favorite，这个单词比较长，教学时要分音节，fa—vo—rite。

(3) 教师边走边带读单词，保证教室每个角落的学生都能听清发音，不要只站在讲台上。如 program 最后是闭口音，教师要让学生看到自己的口型。

(4) 让单个学生尝试着朗读单词。

(5) 比较难发音的单词，在请学生仔细听后，还可以引导学生看自己的口型，将听与看结合，体会正确的发音口型、舌位、唇齿、口型大小等。如 very well，fish，grapes 等。

2. 模仿录音读对话

在此操练中，学生应该注意的以及教师应该指导的重点是：

(1) 一般疑问句用升调，如 Have you bought any oranges? ↗ Is this your book? ↗ 特殊疑问句用降调，如 What do you usually have for lunch? ↘教学时教师可用手势来引导学生发音。

(2) 注意每句话中单词的连续失去爆破，如 The parents listened to the school choir at three ten in the hall. They had tea and cakes。

(3) 注意复合句中按意群进行的适当停顿，如 I see a few parents，(P) some teachers and a lot of students (P) when I'm walking to school. 区分不了意群，学生在齐读时就会出现读不整齐的现象（P 表示停顿）。

(4) 注意每句话中的重音，突出要表达的主要意思，如 These are ˈapples。

(5) 陈述句出现并列的单词或短语时，and 前面的单词或短语一般都用升调，最后一个用降调，如 I have a book，↗ a pen ↗ and a bag。↘

(三) 听音示意

该操练环节是指听录音或教师说出的内容，学生做出相应的反应，如听听做做 (listen and do)，听听指指 (listen and point)，听听画画 (listen and draw)，听听涂涂 (listen and color)，等等。这些都是学生感兴趣的练习，不仅轻松愉快，而且能反映学生对新知识的掌握情况。

案例1

教师在教授了新句型Look at…，What color is it，It's…后，让学生在纸上分别画出学过的四个物品，a boat，a balloon，a flower，a kite，然后涂上他们喜欢的颜色，并用刚学的新句型来向大家介绍他们的作品。

学生根据自己所画、所涂的物品流利地说出了："Look at the boat. It's orange，yellow and blue."

学生们还可以两两对话：

S1：Look at the kite.

S2：What color is it?

S1：It's blue. It's beautiful.

学生们充分发挥他们的想象力，在轻松愉快的氛围中用英语自如地表达了自己的情感。毫无疑问，这样的操练是成功的。

案例2

在学了词组take out后，教师可以通过听听做做的方式来进行操练。请一位同学上讲台，教师说英语，学生做动作。教师说："Open your school bag. Take out a ruler. Take out two books. Take out three pens. Take out four pencils. Take out a skipping rope."学生依次完成。

在教授了介词in之后，教师也可以通过听听做做来进行操练。教师说英语，学生做动作。教师可以说："Put your rubber in your pencil case. Put your math book in your school bag."此外，教师还可以想出更新奇的想法，比如，Put your hand in your pocket. Put your finger in your mouth. 还可以让学生自己说、自己做，这样效果会更好。

（四）听与写结合

听与写结合也是有效的操练方法，如听音连线（listen and connect），听音标号（listen and number），听音打钩（listen and tick），等等。教师可通过这三种方法来帮助学生熟悉新学的单词或句型。

1. 听音连线

将听到的句子与相应的图片连起来。

(1)

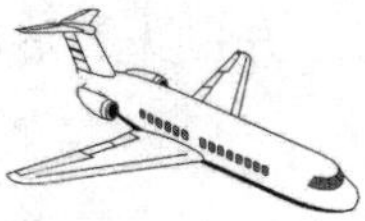

(2)

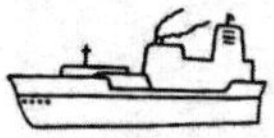

2. 听音标号

(1) 将听到的句子标上正确的序号。

Let's eat the birthday cake.	(1)
How many balloons?	(5)
Can I have some chicken?	(2)
I like hamburgers.	(4)
Have some fresh fries.	(3)

(2) 根据录音内容给图片标上正确的序号。

(6)　(2)　(4)　(5)　(3)　(1)

squirrel　elephant　cat　panda　mouse　birds

3. 听音打勾

听音打勾，选出和你所听到的相符合的图片。

There is a library near our school.

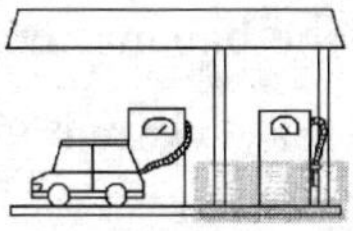

( )　(√)　( )　( )

（五）听与说结合

英语学习中听与说本来就是相辅相成、密不可分的。只有听懂，才能说清楚，才能表情达意，从而充分发挥语言的交际作用。教师可以通过以下方法进行操练：利用多媒体，让学生听与新知识相关的新语言材料，训练学生捕捉重要的信息，并口头表达出来。这种操练通常包含三个步骤。

1. 听前活动

在听新的语言材料前，教师要帮助学生确立听的方向和目的，使学生能主动预测未知的信息。听前活动包括讨论有关的话题、预测材料内容、复述要点等。教师要启发学生带着任务去听，同时让学生用自己的语言来组织听到的信息并回答问题。这样既锻炼了学生的思维能力，又培养了学生的口头表达能力。

2. 听中活动

这部分包括总体理解、抓住关键词和实时记笔记等。听的最终目的是理解句子、篇章，所以在听的过程中，一定要重点训练学生抓住句子中的关键词和段落的主题句。让学生把已听懂并理解的部分作为线索，联系上下文猜测尚未听懂理解的部分。另外，在听的过程中适当地记笔记也是必不可少的，如记下时间、地点、人物、数字等内容，这些内容往往是听力材料的关键。

3. 听后活动

听后活动也很重要，它是教师引导学生回顾听的过程中遇到的问题并寻找解决问题的方法，帮助学生找出弱点，建议补救方法的活动。如让学生找出听不懂词的原因（比如无法辨音、无法快速反应或不懂生词），然后在稍后的操练中解决相应的问题。这样一来，有诊断性质的听后活动作为听说操练的必不可少的一个环节，把纯粹的听说训练变成了技巧培养和听说训练相结合的练习，使听说操练落到实处。

案例 1

听录音中的故事

Mocky's Bad Day

Mocky goes to school by car. But yesterday he went to school by bus. After school, he visited Ann's house. He sat at the table. He ate the banana. Ann's mother came into the kitchen. Suddenly Mocky couldn't breath. Because he ate the banana too quickly. Ann hit him on the back. He wasn't sick any more. Next day Mocky visited Ann again. He came into the kitchen. But he didn't eat any more.

活动设计：

（1）听前活动：教师让学生看 PPT 上的图片并提问：What did Mocky do yesterday?

教师给出几幅图可以给学生多一些空间思考，有利于在听前激活学生的思维并促使学生联想。这些联想会使学生对要听的内容和相关词汇有一定的了解。

（2）听中活动：教师要让学生多听录音，至少听两遍，并在听的过程中让学生记下关键信息，如 visited Ann's house，sat at the table，ate the banana，couldn't breath，too quickly，hit him on the back，wasn't sick，next day，didn't eat any more。因为此操练旨在复习过去时态，教师可通过如下问题使学生加深对过去时读音和拼写的印象：

What did Mocky do yesterday?

(He visited Ann's house.)

Where did he sit?

(He sat at the table.)

What did Mocky eat?

(He ate a banana.)

Why was he sick?

(Because he ate the banana too quickly and couldn't breath.)

Who hit him on the back?

(Ann.)

Did he eat more the next day?

(No，he didn't.)

（3）听后活动：教师可以让学生把 PPT 上的图描述出来，通过说来体会过去时的用法，形成正确的读音，以此加强对动词过去时结构特点的感悟。如果学生有困难或表达错误，给他们再听一遍的机会。

二、听的游戏

在操练环节，教师要通过设计有趣、多样的游戏紧紧“抓住”学生的耳朵。

1. 二人转（Turn and turn）

游戏说明：两位学生各持一张单词卡片，听教师口令做动作，同时互相观看对方手中的单词卡片，看哪一位同学能以最快的速度认出另一位同学手中的卡片。

2. 狼来了（The wolf is coming）

游戏说明：学生围成一圈，当听到教师事先约定的一个单词时向自己的座位跑去，慢的学生就会被教师抓住。为保证安全，人多时可分组进行。

3. 猜声音（Guess the sound）

游戏说明：教师请一位学生背对同学，另一位同学拍打这位同学的小手并说出单词，回座后，请这位同学猜是哪一位同学，用于单词的操练或句型的练习。

4. 传声筒（Whisper）

游戏说明：可用于分组游戏，两组同学传不同的句子，看哪组传得又快又好，可以设置奖励。

5. 下命令（Up and down）

游戏说明：五六个人拿新单词卡上前站成一圈，老师下第一个命令，如 apple，手拿此卡片的学生马上边下蹲边说 apple down，apple down，apple down，banana down. 那么手拿 banana 卡片的学生马上下蹲并说自己的指令，然后再给别人下指令。

6. 听名字（Whose name?）

游戏说明：老师和学生一起拍手说单词或句子，当老师突然喊学生名字时，被喊到名字的学生马上起立说出该单词或句子，老师在喊名字的同时手指另外一位学生，如果被指到的学生起立就会被扣分。

7. 心有灵犀（Say and do）

游戏说明：当学过两三个单词后，两个同学站前边，听到指令后，两人同时转一圈并同时说出一词，若说出同样的词就获胜，否则不得分。

8. 耳听八方（Listening and hearing）

游戏说明：老师选定一位学生面对黑板站立，同时悄悄找数个学生说词或句子，之后那个学生转头猜有几人说了词或句子，每次找的人不能太多，四五个为宜。

9. 找物品（Where is it?）

游戏说明：把五件不同颜色的物品放成一排。给学生几秒钟记住每个颜色物品所放的位置。点一位学生上来，蒙住他的眼睛，用英语告诉他“Find the blue…”。学生根据自己的记忆，走向相应的颜色的物品，并将它拿起。

10. 贪吃蛇（Gluttonous snake）

游戏说明：设置一个简单的问题，如 What's your favorite fruit? 然后请学生 1 回答，学生 1 回答后，学生 2 要复述学生 1 的回答，再给出自己的回答，接着，学生 3 要复述学生 1 和学生 2 的回答，再给出自己的回答，依此类推。

T：What's your favorite fruit?

S1：My favorite fruit is apple.

S2：His/Her favorite fruit is…. My favorite fruit is….

S3：His/Her favorite fruit is…. His/Her favorite fruit is…. My favorite fruit is….

最后谁记得最多，谁就获胜。该游戏也可以在小组中进行，不仅练习了句型，也训练了学生的听力，而且激发了学生的学习兴趣，达到了在玩中学、在活动中练的目的。

第二节　说的操练

语言作为一种人际交流的工具，最直接的呈现就是口语和书面语。相对于阅读是跟随作者的思路去被动感知而言，口语则是一种主动的表达，教师要通过创设不同的情境使学生将已学的知识在情境中呈现出来。

一、说的形式

在操练环节，教师可通过模拟性说、交际性说、创造性说这三种形式来进行操练。

（一）模拟性说

模拟性说可以采取以下方法展开：

1. 双向式操练（同桌或前后）

案例

让学生用“is”“are”来进行物品的描述，可采用“你说我猜”的方式，主要过程如下：教师为学生在大屏幕上展示了许多表示动物、食品和地点的图片，首先让学生根据教师的示范进行同桌活动，然后找单个学生来描述，其他学生则需要认真去听，根据描述进行猜测，学生会表现出极高的热情，积极参与。在这个活动中，首先展开的是同桌活动，然后进行单个学生的描述，虽然进行描述的学生是有限的，但其余学生也有明确的任务：捕捉信息，进行猜测，并用“Is it…?”来进行互动和交流。学生在生动、有趣的活动中巩固如何运用“is”“are”来描述物品，每个学生都有机会直接进行活动体验，参与学习活动的积极性得以提高，并且在活动的过程中，学生可以根据自身知识的掌握情况，灵活控制语言的使用情况。能力强一些的学生可以运用自己的语言，能力稍差一些的学生可尽量运用课本提供的语言，这体现了活动的灵活性。

2. 小组式操练（前后左右4人或8人）

案例

猜猜纸上画的动作：引导学生利用新学的句子 Can you sing/swim/…？来提问，用 Yes，I can/No，I can't. 来回答。可以采取小组式操练，即 Chain game（ask and answer one by one）。

3. 纵向式操练（按座位往后纵向连锁操练）

4. 横向式操练（按座位横向连锁操练）

换用模拟操练的不同形式可以激发说的兴趣，但真正要把模拟操练练活，教师还得融入学生之中，要给学生准备练习材料，引导练习，在学生分组练习时要注意巡回观察，辅助困难学生，有时还需要与学生进行双向交流以充分调动学生参加口头操练的积极性。师生间不同形式的口头操练是学生掌握语言结构和排除心理障碍并得以开口的必要活动。

（二）交际性说

交际性说主要是通过创设情境使学生达到操练的目的。

1. 创设情境时要给学生说的机会

语言教学情境也就是语言交际的社会情境。语言离开了情境就失去了它的意义。在操练环节中创设情境的作用在于：首先，它可以满足小学生的心理需要，引起学生的有意注意，明白学习英语是为交际服务的；其次，情境是各种活动的依托，能使活动生动化、趣味化、真实化。学生在真实或接近真实的情景中操练，会学得更快、记得更牢。利用情境操练语言，可以进一步加深学生对语言的理解，加深对语言知识的熟悉程度，从而能使学生更好地运用语言。

（1）创设的情境要有针对性，且呈递进式。

有些老师的操练形式比较单一、机械。有这样一个案例：老师为了操练 Do you like…？这一新学句型，向全班每位同学提问：Do you like basketball？这样的操练就显得过于枯燥。也许老师认为自己应该面向全体，却忽略了操练的情境设计。泛泛、单调的情境使学生无法得到有效的操练。因此，情境的多样化设计就显得尤为重要，它能使操练变得活泼、有趣，引起学生的注意。但是情境的设计也不要太复杂，要有针对性。因为一堂课只有40分钟，如果情境过于复杂，没有针对性，操练就会失去意义。学生需要一段时间去熟悉一个情境，然后再跳到下一个情境，情境太多，容易使教学脱离大纲，造成只有部分学生达到要求。

有的老师认为好的操练只要有某个情境就行了，于是操练中情境呈累积式出现，一个情境接一个情境，这些情境之间缺乏联系。其实情境之间应呈递进式。比如操练 I like…和 I don't like…，如果教师前面设计了 Guessing game，让学生猜一猜喜欢的事物，那么后面的情境就应进一步强化，以提高学生的说话能力。可以设计一个 supermarket 的场景，让学生画两个篮子，一个放自己喜欢的物品，另一个放自己不喜欢的物品，然后让他告诉别人自己喜欢什么、不喜欢什么，请别的学生帮他放好。

（2）创设的情境要考虑说的交际功能。

口语是有声的语言，是言语的输出或释放过程。说是在听的基础上发展起来的。

有的老师缺乏用语观念，他们认为，在说的操练环节，学生能“说”这个句子就等于操练成功。事实上，脱离了情境，话语就不具备交际功能。如在不同的情境中，“Ok”可以是同意，也可以表达征求意见，还可以是威胁。说的操练应以语义在情境中的实现为设计原则，尽量以真实的语言交际替代机械操练，让学生在真实的或模拟真实的交际场合中进行语言操练。虽然为了熟悉句子结构的机械操练是有必要的，但是在机械操练时教师也可以创设情境，让机械操练不那么机械。

案例 1

在学习了句型 What's your name? I am…后，教师设计一个“百变的我”活动，即可以解决情境问题。活动准备：每人准备若干张小纸片，每张上写一个自己崇拜的人的名字，反盖纸片于桌面。开展活动：两人一组问答比赛。每人抽一张纸片，自己就拥有了一个新的名字。在限定的时间内比赛，看哪一组“变身”最多。这样，一个“真实”的情境就出现了，而且加入了比赛的元素，学生的兴趣加大，活动更投入，操练更有效。

案例 2

在学习了句型 When were you born? I was born in…后，模仿案例 1，也可以创设出一个类似的情境——“百变的我”，只是变化的是自己的生日月份。活动准备：每人 12 张小纸片，每张上写一个月份，反盖纸片于桌面。开展活动：两人一组问答比赛。每人抽一张纸片，自己就拥有了一个新的生日月份。在限定的时间内猜对方的生日月份，比赛看哪一组在限定时间内猜到的最多。因为要猜月份，当然就得用上上述目标句型了。

2. 创设的情境要促进学生语言与想象力的发展

培养学生的观察、记忆、思维、想象能力和创新精神是英语课程的任务之一。小学生具有丰富的想象力，教师应在操练环节中巧设情境，激发学生的想象力，培养其创新精神。想象情境虽不像实体情境那样看得见、摸得着，但它的意象却比实体情境更深远，更富有感情色彩。学生的情绪往往在想象情境中得到调动，其想象力得到充分发挥，语言能力也得以提升。

案例

学生在学习了现在进行时态后，教师可以试着与学生一起来想象正发生在丛林里的事，和学生们一起编故事。孩子的想象力是值得我们敬佩的。大家你一言、我一语，竟然编成了这样的故事：It is a sunny day. In the forest，the birds are singing. A bird is swinging. The giraffe is dancing. The rabbits are running. The monkey is jumping. The elephant is walking. The mouse is running. The cat is running. The cat is catching the mouse. The snake is eating a rabbit. The fish is swimming. The frog is singing. …

3. 创设情境需要时常更换教学手段

让学生保持新鲜感，是防止学生产生厌学心理的良方。如果教师在操练环节不更换教学手段或形式，学生的学习兴致就不高，他们会感到索然无味，产生不愿说的倾向。所以教师要利用挂图、录音机、多媒体、简笔画、歌曲、游戏、童谣等多种形式组织说的操练。让学生带着欲望去操练，每到操练环节心里就想着老师这次会有什么新花样呢？这样，教师操练的目的就达到了。

（1）视听情境。

在英语操练中，“视”和“听”是常用的教学手段。按照我国英语课程标准的要求，在小学阶段，特别是低、中年级，一定要贯彻“听说领先”的教学原则，要把“激发和培养学生学习英语的兴趣，使学生树立自信心，养成良好的学习习惯和形成有效的学习策略，发展自主学习的能力和合作精神”这一目标放在首位。因此，在说的操练过程中，教师可以通过创设视听情境充分调动学生使用新知识的热情。在创设视听情境时，教师可以充分利用多媒体技术，因为多媒体技术不仅能够创设逼真的各种情景，而且能化无声为有声，化静为动，化抽象为具体，可以有效地综合利用学生的听觉、视觉等多种感官，提高操练效率。

案例 1

在《开心学英语》Book 2 Unit 1 Animals 的操练环节中，学生要操练的是有关动物的单词以及几个简单的动词。为了充分调动学生操练的积极性，教师可以创设一个这样的情境：多媒体中出现一个动物园的图片，每个区域的动物先遮挡住，让学生根据动物的叫声说出这是什么动物，接着多媒体展示中国地图，让大家乘飞机去到不同的地方，了解各个地方的动物。飞机飞到某一个地方，多媒体中播放声音：“Hello，Welcome here! I'm a crane.”同时呈现动物画面。接下来到其他各处，请同学们根据画面逐一介绍。同样的方法还可用于动词 fly，run，swim 等的教学。学生在这样一种视听情境中，始终保持着积极的求知欲和学习兴趣。

(2) 生活情境。

在操练中模拟学生熟悉的生活情境，给学生提供生活中熟悉的词汇和语言材料，让学生在熟悉的情境中操练新知识，能促使其更好地理解和运用词汇、句型。

案例 1

在操练《开心学英语》Book 2 Unit 10 How Many Are There 中的 thirteen，fourteen，fifteen，sixteen，seventeen，eighteen，nineteen，twenty 这些数字单词时，教师可以设置这样一个生活情境：我的农场大丰收了，但是我忙不过来了，大家一起来帮我数一数我的果实和我养的动物吧。然后整个操练围绕帮助老师数数而进行。在整个环节中，先数动物，复习学过的个位数字，后出示动物的图片，让学生识别，复习旧单词。接下来，让学生数出更多的单词。最后，学生间的问答以及帮助教师统计数量等活动都围绕该情境展开。

案例 2

在操练《英语》(PEP 版) 五年级上册 Unit 3 What's Your Favorite Food? 中的新单词 sweet，sour，salty，hot 时，教师考虑到这几个单词都属于味道单词，就准备了四个黑色的瓶子，里面分别装了四种味道的水，请学生尝一尝。学生要根据味道做出表情，也可以做出各种假象，再请其他学生来猜这是何种味道。这个操练环节是学生们生活中再熟悉不过的味觉体验，因此学生们兴趣浓厚，参与的积极性非常高，大家都抢着要说，操练的效果自然不言而喻了。

案例 3

在《英语》(PEP 版) 六年级上册 Unit 3 What Are You Going to Do 的课中，教师在进行完课文的导入和讲解之后，结合即将到来的“六一”儿童节，为学生设计了一个调查性的任务，调查小组成员的“六一”计划：Where are you going to go? When are you going to go? Who are you going to go with? What are you going to do?

然后，学生要结合调查结果进行汇报：

He's/She's going to…，学生在进行反馈的同时实现了人称的有效拓展。在这个活动中，教师创设了“谈六一计划”的生活化情境。在操练中，学生不是在被动地进行机械操练，而是在情境中主动地实践和体验。这样的操练贴近学生的生活，同时也体现了语言的交际功能，有利于提高教学效率。

语言源于生活。没有了生活中的情境，操练会显得枯燥无味。在教师创设的情境中，学生可以通过生活经验，主动运用所学词汇、句型。通过创设的生活情境，学生懂得了在生活中如何运用所学有效提高交际能力。

（三）创造性说

创造性说可以通过看图说话、编故事、编唱歌曲等来实现。

1. 看图说话

小学生注意力不稳定，如果一堂课围绕几幅呆板的图进行讨论，学生很快就会失去兴趣。此时教师再创设一个与图片类似的情景，配上音乐和道具，学生又可以活跃起来。

案例 1

在看图说话时，教师可以设计一些疑点启发学生的思维，教师用自己的一勺水，引出了学生的一桶水，以至无穷之水。

师：图片上有什么？

生：鸟 bird（表述公母对小学生而言过难，可以用自己会的 boy，girl 表示）。

师：特征是什么？

数量：2 只 two birds。

颜色：1 只红色 one red bird（one bird is red），1 只绿色 one green bird（one bird is green），很漂亮 very beautiful。

位置：站在树上 stand in a tree。

行为：它们在做什么？（这个可以有很多种设想）（1）它们站在树上，谈恋爱。They stand in the tree. They love each other.（2）它们在亲吻，它们相爱了。They are kissing. They love each other.（3）它们在谈论……（编一段对话）。比如，The green bird says："My dear，I love you." The red bird says："I love you too." 学生可能会有更丰富的想象。

结果怎样呢？它们很幸福。They are very happy.

最后，学生会这样描述这幅图：

On Saturday morning，it's sunny and warm. There are two beautiful birds standing in a tree. One bird is green. He is a boy. One bird is red. She is a girl. The green bird says："Oh my dear，I love you very much." The red bird says："I love you too." … They are very happy!

案例 2

在看图说话时，教师可以不规定形式，让学生自由发挥。学生可以两人一组，充分发挥想象力把对话拓展开来。这种操练把学生从书本上引导到生活中来，实现了从知识向技能的转化。

Talk about the picture in at least 5 sentences. Begin your talk with the sentence given below.

用至少 5 句话描述图片，以下列句子开始。

Tom, who is very short, is playing basketball with his tall classmate Dick.

案例 3

通过猜谜进行创造性看图说话。在教授物品时，教师可以出谜语，让学生边看物品图边猜谜。如，I have a good friend. It has no head and no arms. It has four legs and a back, but it can't walk. What is it? 在教师的解释和暗示下，学生很快猜到了“chair”。然后教师再给出“bed”“table”“egg”“doll”等图，让学生自编谜语，进一步激发学生的学习兴趣，巩固教学效果。

2. 编故事

编故事的活动实施应当遵循循序渐进的发展原则，一般来说，学生应当经历四个水平，即词汇水平、短语水平、句子水平、短文水平。但是，即使是词汇水平，也不是机械地填词，学生头脑中要有全篇故事。不管学生怎么编，都不能脱离故事，都要涉及故事的构思。

（1）完成故事。

这是最初级的编故事。教师先提供故事的基本材料，然后有两种做法：第一，只要求编所缺的信息；第二，基于已知的故事情节，根据自己的想象增加故事情节。

案例

教师口述故事素材：

The baby mice want to go out. They want to see things outside the hole. The mother mouse says to them: “Just wait a minute. Let me look.” The mother mouse looks out of the hole. She says to her children: “You can't go out now. There are four cats in the room. They want to catch us and eat us." "But I can't see them," the youngest mouse says to her mother. "Look!" the mother mouse says, "there is a white cat under the table, a brown cat behind the door, a black cat beside the flowers and a white-black cat just near the hole."

然后让学生根据提示试着讲故事。

There are four cats in the room. There is a ________ cat under the table, a ________ cat behind the door, a ________ cat beside the flowers and a ________ cat just near the hole.

（2）续编故事。

教师选择一个完整的故事，条件是此故事比较适合续编。

故事素材：

Li Ming is a polite boy. He lives in a big house. People usually have a walk after dinner in summer. Li Ming smiles and says hello to them. People think he is a good child. He often sees an old man when he has a walk. He smiles and says hello to him, but he never answers.

Li Ming thinks about the problem. He asks about the old man and he gets to know the old man's birthday. When the old man's birthday comes, he gives him a birthday card. The old man is very happy. They become good friends. The old man is a very famous writer. He writes a story about Li Ming and publishes it in a newspaper. Everybody in the small town knows Li Ming is a polite and kind boy.

教师把故事素材的结尾去掉，让学生续编这个小故事。

教学实施：

A. 在讲故事之前，教师先提供故事的图画，让学生对故事的环境和任务有一个粗略的认识。

B. 教师讲故事。

C. 教师提出问题：Why doesn't the old man give an answer to Li Ming?

D. 小组讨论这个问题。

E. 在小组内部，学生用英语提出假设的故事结局。

F. 各组交流续编的故事结局。

G. 教师组织学生对续编的故事进行评价。

(3) 改编故事。

教师选择适当的故事，提供文本或图画，然后提出改编的具体要求，由学生进行改编。

故事素材：

Mary is not good at Math. One day, she meets a fairy. She asks the fairy to help her. "I can help you. Here is a rose. When you do homework, just ask the rose. It can help you do everything you want it to do with Math." Mary is very happy. Now Mary has a Math puzzle: there are two columns of numbers below:

①	④
②	⑤
③	⑥
⑦	⑨
⑧	24
21	

Can you make the two columns add up to the same total? Remember that you can only move one disk and not remove any other.

Mary does not want to use her head. So she asks the rose. The rose says, "It's very easy. Please the 9 to a 6. Both columns add up to 21." Mary writes down the answer. And then she asks the rose to tell her every answer to the following Math puzzles. She gets good scores.

The final test comes. She brings the rose with her. But she cannot ask the rose any questions. This time, she fails in the Math test.

借助教师的讲解，学生是可以理解这个故事的。教师要求学生改编这个故事，可以提出以下要求：

A. 保持原故事中的人物，但可以增加人物。

B. 不得改动那个能说话的 rose。

C. 可以更换故事中的数学智力题。

3. 编唱歌曲

唱歌是小学生比较喜欢的活动。采用歌曲法进行说的操练，可大大吸引学生的注意力。在操练环节中，教师可以灵活多变，设计“改编歌曲”“改编歌词”等活动，增强活动的趣味性，同时还能让学生进行自主探索、合作，培养学生的想象力。

案例 1

教师要求学生用今天所学的 12 个月份单词来“改编歌词”，将 12 个月份单词填入自己所会的歌曲中，并唱出来（学生一听便表现出了极大的兴趣，主动开始找同学一起商讨、填词、编歌）。几分钟过后，教师告诉大家，他自编了一首（教师将这 12 个单词填入了《友谊地久天长》的曲中）想唱给大家听，如果大家喜欢，教师就教大家唱。歌词如下：

Should auld acquaintance (January) be forgot
and never brought to mind.
Should auld acquaintance (February) be forgot
And days of auld lang syne?
For auld lang syne, my friends
For auld lang syne.
We'll take a cup of kindness yet,
For auld lang syne.
Twa acquaintance be forgot.
And never brought to mind?
Should auld acquaintance (March) be forgot
And days of auld lang syne?
For auld lang syne, my friends
For auld lang syne.
We'll take a cup of kindness yet,
For auld lang syne.

紧接着反复轮唱四遍，每一遍填入 3 个月份单词，这样既学会了这首耳熟能详的苏格兰民歌，又有效操练了 12 个月的月份单词，真可谓一举两得。

案例 2

在教了时间的表达法，如“It's…o'clock.”后，让同学们唱一首“Cuckoo Clock”：

My uncle has cuckoo clock to tell us of the time.
He pops out of his little house and always signs this rhyme (cuckoo, cuckoo).
The cuckoo said it's two o'clock.
He's telling us the time (cuckoo, cuckoo, cuckoo).
The cuckoo said it's three o'clock.
He's telling us the time (cuckoo, cuckoo, cuckoo, cuckoo).

The cuckoo said it's four o'clock.

He's telling us the time (cuckoo, cuckoo… repeat 12 times).

The cuckoo said it's twelve o'clock.

He's telling us the time. He's telling us the time.

教师在教唱这首歌曲时制作了布谷鸟（cuckoo）形状的时钟教具和“uncle”的头饰。然后，教师戴着“uncle”的头饰，手举着布谷鸟形状的时钟，边唱边用手拨动时钟的时针，转到“two”时，教师用食指和中指的手势显示“two”并模仿布谷鸟发出“cuckoo, cuckoo”的声音，这样就增强了歌曲的形象性，唤起了学生的丰富想象。歌曲其他段落的演唱方式以此类推。当教师示范一次后，教师让学生跟着说歌曲的主要句型“It's… o'clock”和数字1～12。在组织学生演唱时，教师可以把学生分成两大组，一组说“The cuckoo said it's twelve o'clock.”，另一组说“He's telling us the time (cuckoo, cuckoo).”。通过几次练习后，教师让学生自己设计动作来演唱这首歌曲，最后请几组学生表演。

二、说的游戏

说的游戏可以使枯燥的学习“言语符号”活动变成玩的“声音游戏”。

1. 大小声（Opposite tune）

游戏说明：学生与教师进行唱反调的游戏，教师声音大，学生声音小；教师声音小，学生的声音相应变大，可用于单词或简单句型的操练。

2. 木头人（Wooden child）

游戏说明：教师或一位学生背对其他人进行单词操练，当教师或学生转过身时其他学生保持原来的动作变成木头人。

3. 传球（Pass the ball）

游戏说明：适用于句子、单词的操练，学生边说边传球，当老师说 stop 时，球在谁手里谁就要快速站起来说三次刚才念的词或句子。

4. 考老师（Guess and say）

游戏说明：找学生到前面，背对着同学拿单词卡，老师来猜，猜对了，同学一起读；猜错了，同学一起告诉老师。

5. 排雷（Where is the bomb?）

游戏说明：老师准备 20 个左右的乒乓球，其中半数标明是雷。平均装到两个非透明的口袋中。每组找一位同学到前面来比赛，看哪一组能在限定的时间内（可让学生说新单词 10 遍）先把雷排除掉。

6. 邮递员（Postman）

游戏说明：准备两套可拼成句子的单词卡，每组选派两位同学当邮递员，老师把两套卡打乱。看哪组能最先拼出完整的句子，就像邮递员要把每封信正确地送到每一家一样，其余学生在下面说句子，此游戏适合句子操练。

7. 猜价格（How much is it?）

游戏说明：找一位同学到前面来猜价格，老师给出一个数字，让其他同学在下面提示。比如，lower 与 higher，看其能否在限定的时间内猜出来，此游戏适合反义词操练以及比较级单词的操练。

8. 过山车（Get on the train）

游戏说明：学生们手拉手围成圈边走边说要操练的句子或单词，老师和一个圈里的学生手撑手扣住哪个学生，哪个学生需说出所操练的句子或词。

9. 接力赛（Relay race）

游戏说明：将学生分成较为平均的两组。每组按顺序进行抢答，获胜的坐下，输的要站着和下一个学生比赛，哪组最先全部都坐下即为冠军。

10. 传传看（Pass the word）

游戏说明：用于操练句子。每人说一个单词，最后一个人说整句话，看哪组速度快。如：where are you going? 每人说一个单词，“where”“are”“you”“going”最后一个人说：“where are you going?”

第三节　读的操练

读是辨认文字符号并将文字符号转换为有意义的信息输入的能力。读的操练对提高英语阅读理解能力、养成良好的阅读习惯非常重要。读的操练是增长见识学问、改变思维习惯、修身养性的一个复杂的心理和智力活动。

英语学习需要不断地复现，需要大量地输入来强化所学的知识并加以拓展。在读的操练中，简单机械地复现和输入会使学生失去学习的兴趣，只有将所学的知识放到新的情境中，放到新的阅读活动中才能吸引学生，使学生保持持久的学习兴趣。

一、读的形式

在操练环节，教师可采用认读、朗读、阅读等形式来进行操练。

（一）认读

“认读”在英语教学中用 recognition 这个词表示。《朗文语言教学及应用语言学辞典》

对 recognition 这个词是这样解释的：所谓 recognition，就是指辨认出某一个单词或者一个词组是否曾经见过，并且能够指出它的基本词意。比如你看到“duck”，就知道是鸭子的意思，这就是认读了。认读和记忆单词两者比较，认读稍微容易一些。

案例 1

教学目标 A：学生能够听、说、读、写本课所学单词

教学目标 B：学生能够听、说、认读本课所学单词

相对来讲，教学目标 B 的制定者对认读目标更为关注，明确提出学生应该能听懂某个单词，而且看到某个词或图片要能说出这个单词，进而能认读这个单词。如果在制定教学目标时教师能关注认读能力的培养，那么在设计教学活动时就能安排恰当的活动，学生的认读能力也会得到较好的发展。

案例 2

教师可以把教材上的单词分为生活用品、动物、植物、水果、食物、家庭成员、身体部位、学习用具、交通工具等等，同一类的单词放在一起给学生认读和记忆。如将 mango，lemon，sofa，coffee，jeep，chocolate，sandwich，pizza，hamburger 等词（其对应的中文都是音译外来词）放在一起让学生认读。

案例 3

教师可以通过对比使认读变得更为有效。如近义词 father—Dad，mother—Mum 等，反义词 long—short，bad—good 等，再如形近词 there—these，chair—hair 等。操练 smooth 这个单词时，可以先复习学过的 tooth 这个词，通过这两个单词的比较，印象就更深刻了。

（二）朗读

朗读在读的操练中占有十分重要的位置，它不仅可以使小学生在各种朗读中感受英语的语音、语调和节奏，培养学生的英语语感，还可以使小学生的听觉能力和思维能力得到提高。正确的朗读方式更可以给人以美的享受，进而激发学生学习英语的兴趣，促进英语教学质量的提高。

1. 多方法激发学生的朗读兴趣

激发小学生对英语朗读的兴趣是培养小学生英语朗读能力的首要一步。心理学研究表明，小学生的注意力持续性差，如果不能以趣味吸引学生，学生会在反复的朗读操练中感到枯燥，在朗读前失去信心。因此，教学可以从三方面着手：

（1）教师正确优美的示范。

教师的朗读水平对学生有着直接的影响。教师必须不断学习、练习，以自身优美、纯正的语音、语调感染学生，给学生以美的享受，从而引起学生的朗读欲望。在操练前，教

师运用朗读技巧对课文进行准确生动的朗读能使学生对作品中的人物、事件、景物、地点等产生丰富的联想。教师通过轻重缓急、抑扬顿挫的朗读，能赋予文字生动的意义，还能帮助学生提高口头表达能力和记忆力。

（2）形式多样的课堂朗读。

不要将课堂的朗读操练仅仅当作检查学生是否掌握新知识的手段，这样小学生会失去朗读的乐趣。教师要抓住小学生的心理，针对小学生好动、争强好胜等特点，以及朗读内容的不同，积极运用情景、游戏、奖励等手段，开展形式多样的朗读训练，如听录音跟读、分角色朗读、表演读（根据人物的年龄、职业、性格的不同来读）、“开火车”读、比赛读（男女生赛读、小组赛读、反串读）等，使学生乐于朗读，给学生提供展示的机会，满足学生的表现欲望。

（3）丰富多彩的朗读活动。

为了让学生把“读”当作每天都必须做的一项操练，可以举行丰富多彩的活动。如一单元结束后举行一次“英文朗读比赛”，评选出“英语朗读之星”，获奖的学生必须达到两个条件：第一，每天朗读英语二十分钟，请家长签名确认；第二，在比赛中脱颖而出，有自己的特点。可以将获胜者的照片贴在教室的英语角中。教师可以自行降低比赛的难度，特别是对后进生，让他们感觉到“努力一下也可以获奖”。只有这样，学生才会在丰富多彩的操练中增强对英语朗读的兴趣和信心。

2. 多方面培养学生的朗读习惯

英语课程标准要求学生能在指认物体的前提下认读所学词语；能在图片的帮助下读懂小故事；能根据拼读规律读出简单的单词；能读懂教材中简短的要求或指令；能读懂问候卡等中的简单信息；能借助图片读懂简单的故事或小短文，养成按意群阅读的习惯；能正确朗读所学故事或短文，大声朗读并注意语音、语调。由于小学生的英语学习缺少运用英语进行真实交际的环境，在他们学习的一开始，英语词、形、声、义协调融合还不能熟练掌握的时候，必须加强对小学生英语朗读习惯的培养。这就需要教师在操练中，把好语音关，严格要求，适度纠音，持之以恒，帮学生切实打好语音、语调基础。英语朗读要有正确的读音跟语调，必须多读多练，即要求学生在朗读过程中养成正确理解、准确模仿、深刻体会、主动表达的学习习惯。

（1）培养学生听录音跟读的良好习惯。

与教材配套的录音带大多是由英、美等外籍人士录制而成的，其语音语调自然、地道、规范。对于初学英语的小学生来说，应尽可能地多听、多模仿，增强感性认识，把好英语的“入门关”。然而，单纯地听录音比较枯燥，自控能力较差的小学生很容易注意力不集中，教师可以在操练中采取各种方法和手段吸引学生的注意力，培养他们善于听录音的习惯，有时教师可以将操练延伸到课外。教师可以充分发挥家长资源，开展“我和爸爸

(妈妈) 比英语”的活动，激起学生听录音的动机。有些家长英语比较好，在听录音跟读的过程中可以指出孩子模仿时存在的问题，使孩子能精益求精；有些家长虽然没有英语基础，但能激发孩子的自豪感，从而使孩子获得成功的体验。小学生模仿力强，如果他们能坚持听录音跟读，并自觉地将自己的读音与标准规范的音调进行对比，纠正自己音调上的错误，那么这将为他们打好语音、语调的良好基础。

(2) 培养学生大声朗读的良好习惯。

为了不至于学成“哑巴英语”和“聋子英语”，教师应要求学生读出声来。其实，大声朗读的作用还不止于此，心理学研究表明，大声朗读时不仅需要用脑，还需要同时动用自己的发音器官和听觉器官，这样能够使注意力集中，加速记忆；大声朗读还有助于培养学生学习英语的自信心。因此，教师应不断地提醒学生在朗读时大声、有感情，切莫漫不经心。当然也不提倡声嘶力竭地朗读，这样反而会影响注意力、体力，削弱记忆和理解，不利于持久学习。

(3) 培养学生眼到、口到、心到的良好朗读习惯。

受儿童年龄特征的限制，小学生的朗读往往随心所欲，一听到教师或录音的示范发音就急于开口模仿，轻声跟着读了，但往往发音也不准确，还会影响其他学生听课。因此，要训练学生仔细听教师的示范发音，提醒学生边听边观察教师的口形，然后再模仿。在模仿的过程中要求学生口、眼与大脑并用，做到眼到、口到、心到。刚开始，学生可能很难达到这个要求，教师可以先要求学生做到“眼到-口到”，逐步达到“口到-心到”。对于低年级学生，可以先让学生进行指读，读到哪里，指到哪里，训练学生集中注意力，渐渐养成眼、口、心一致的好习惯。

著名语言学家奈达说，要想在语言如何搭配方面建立可靠的语感，就必须反复听、反复说，没有别的办法可替代。在操练中培养小学生良好的英语朗读习惯也不是一朝一夕的事，只有持之以恒，不断摸索新的朗读训练方法，正确引导学生坚持朗读训练，才能提高学生的朗读能力。

3. 多角度训练学生的朗读技巧

在小学阶段不管哪个年级，都应当重视读的操练。有效的朗读指导能使学生从中受感染，并能调动他们学习的积极性，对学生养成良好的朗读习惯和阅读习惯都能起到很好的促进作用。

案例 1

手掌向上向下指导升降调

在教学句子“Are the horses?”“No, they aren't.”“Are they donkeys? ”“Yes, they are.”和长句“I see three geese, five cats, two pigs, two dogs and eight rabbits.”时，教师首先通过在句子上标注升降调的方式，给予学生最直观的感知，进而结合手势，给予学生清晰和到位的示范，再通过学生齐读，分组读，个别读，检查是否朗读正确，让学生在潜移默化的熏陶中去感悟英语的语音语调，获得朗读的初步技能。

案例 2

手指一上一下指导重读弱读

英语是一种听起来悦耳动听的语言，它有像汉语一样的节奏。我们知道汉语中的一些词汇在口语中是轻读的而不是重读的，如“我们的同学”中的“的”字是不会重读的。同样，英语的节奏通常也与音节相关联。如 'Catch the 'ball.（强/弱/强），I 'think so.（弱/强/弱）。英语中的轻读和重读使其如一首音韵和谐婉转的诗歌。例如在教学《新标准英语》（外研社版，简称“NSE”）Book 8 时，让学生通过重音符号和一上一下手势的帮助，来朗读重点句子“The 'ducks are 'eating our 'picnic.”和“The 'balloons are 'flying a'way.”。从字里行间，训练句子的重读弱读。

案例 3

斜杠断句指导意群

引导学生注意词组的含义，按意群朗读，让朗读的内容情景化、意义化，使学生边读边理解边记忆。小学生的朗读容易产生一词一顿，无停顿地连续，自由停顿而读破句等现象。在课堂上要引导学生划分词组，训练学生掌握句子停顿的能力，运用画斜杠、大量模仿、反复诵读等方式，加深学生对句子的理解。当教师示范朗读时，学生可以在应注意断句处做出标记。如在教学 NSE Book5 M9 时，教师通过“I'm going to/make you a surprise cake/on your birthday.”的断句朗读，降低了难度，也保证了句子不会被读得支离破碎。同时，要留够时间让学生试读、练读；留够时间让学生读出感觉，读出“洋味”。在小学阶段，我们无法跟学生讲明词性，因此我们必须用教师的示范去帮助学生，从而使学生的朗读做到准确流利。

4. 有效利用 Chant，提高学生的朗读技巧

“Chant”是指在教学中有意将所教内容编成朗朗上口的英文儿歌，这可以提高趣味性，拓展课堂内容，训练学生的节奏感和语音语调，提高学生的朗读技巧。为了把操练过程变得轻松、愉快，教师可以给单词添上节奏的鼓槌，让学生在有节奏地、反复地唱或喊叫的过程中操练单词；也可以给句子插上韵律的翅膀，把一些易混或不易记住的短句编成儿歌，将其由朗读简单的语音变成语言操练。

案例 1

Oxford English（上海版）2B Unit 6 中有两个新授单词：hungry，thirsty。在分别示范发音，并让学生跟读之后，可让学生朗读下面的儿歌进行操练：

Mary is hungry,

She's not happy,

No berry，no cherry，

Mary is hungry，

She's not happy.

Betty is thirsty，

She's not happy.

"What do you want，Betty?"

"What do you want，Betty?"

"Water，juice，coffee!"

"Water，juice，coffee!"

Oh! She's very happy!

这首儿歌把 hungry，thirsty 及有关的食品、饮料整合了进去。这样，不仅让学生记住了 hungry，thirsty 这两个单词，还巩固了/ri/和/ti/的发音，同时又帮助学生复习了以前学过的语言知识，即 When we are hungry，we eat something. When we are thirsty，we drink something。

案例 2

《英语》（牛津版）（苏教版）6A Unit 6 的教学主题是 Holidays，课文通过这个主题，让学生了解一些与节日相关的知识，并能用英语表述出来。所以，在操练时，可以用下面的 chant 来总结这单元的教学内容：

Sing and dance，

laugh and play，

eat nice food on New Year's Day.

Go to the hill，

go to the bay，

go to the park on May Day.

"Let's play games." We happily say.

We have a good time on Children's Day.

Dear Mum，China.

案例 3

运用多种感觉器官参与 chant。用耳听、用眼看、用鼻子闻、用手摸，让学生在这些过程中操练英语儿歌。

I love apple.

Apple round，apple red，

Apple juicy，apple sweet.

Apple apple，I love you.

Apple sweet I like to eat.

在操练这首儿歌时，教师可提供红红的大苹果，让学生观察苹果的形状、颜色，尝一尝苹果的味道，画一画苹果的形状，学生在动口、动手、动脑的综合性活动中获得了英语学习的经验。

案例 4

在操练“I like doing…”句型时，可以用下面的 chant：

Like，like，what do you like?

Running，running，I like running.

Like，like，what does he like?

Swimming，swimming，he likes swimming.

Like，like，what does she like?

Fishing，fishing，she likes fishing.

Like，like，what do they like?

Jogging，jogging，they like jogging.

Running，swimming，fishing，jogging.

They are all happy every day.

案例 5

在操练动词 nod，shake 时，可结合 raise，put down 用下面的 chant：

Nod your head，yes，yes，yes.（点三下头）

Shake your head，no，no，no.（摇头）

Raise your hand，one，two，three.（举右手伸手指示 1、2、3）

Put down your hand，one，two，three.（放下右手）

案例 6

在《英语》（牛津版）（上海版）3B Module 2 Unit 1 Animals I like 这一单元里首次出现以/t/发音结尾的词，变复数以后发音为/ts/，以/d/发音结尾的单词，变复数以后发音为/dz/。教材通过 cats，lizards 这两个单词的教授，让学生初步了解/ts/，/dz/的发音。根据教学内容和教学要求，教师在操练环节可以教学生下面的儿歌：

Cats，rabbits，they are my pets.

birds，lizards，they are my friends.

Do you like pets?

Do you like lizards?

Yes！Yes！

I like pets!

They are my friends!

案例 7

在开始学英语时，小学生很难记住单词的音、形、义之间的联系。在操练时可以尝试用儿歌帮助学生解决这一难题。如在要求学生掌握5个国家的人的单词（Japanese，Australian，Canadian，American，Englishman）时，由于这几个词都是多音节词，朗读和记忆都较难掌握。但在这些词中，有4个都以an结尾，有条件构成押韵，于是可以利用儿歌来帮助学生记忆：

Chinese，Chinese，I am Chinese.

Japanese，Japanese，he is Japanese.

Australian，Canadian，they speak English.

American，Englishman，they speak English，too.

学生饶有兴趣地朗读了这段顺口溜后，很快就记住了它们的读音。教师可以在朗读的同时出示相应的国旗，使学生当堂记下几个词的音和义。

在实际操练中，好的chant能够激发学生的学习兴趣，帮助他们理解和记忆。但是在具体运用时，教师应充分考虑教学对象、教学内容、教学目标和教学实际等因素，灵活巧妙地运用和创编各种chant，使其真正成为英语操练环节鲜美的调味剂。

5. 充分利用教材，创设交际氛围

教材是训练学生朗读的第一手材料，教师要多琢磨教材，用最适合的方法针对不同的课文进行朗读训练。沪教版《英语》（牛津版）课文内容丰富多彩，内容都很贴近生活，同时提供了较多的替换练习，这也为培养学生进行有感情地朗读提供了便利。教师可以采取如下方法：

（1）模仿课文对话并做替换练习。

（2）教师给出话题与要求，让学生自编对话。

案例

话题：风和太阳争论：Who is stronger?

The North Wind（W）：Mr. Sun，I want to ask you a question.

The Sun（S）：Please. Mr. Wind.

W：Who is stronger，you or me?

S：I think I am.

W：No，you aren't. I'm stronger than you.

S：But how do we know?

W：It's easy. Look! There is a man over there. He's wearing a coat.

W：I can make him take off his coat. Watch!

(The North Wind blows and blows)

S：Aha，Mr. Wind. You can't make him take off his coat.

W：Sorry. I can't. Can you make him take off his coat?

S：Yes，I can.

(The Sun tries and he shines and shines)

The man felt warmer and warmer. Finally he took off his coat.

W：Oh，you're stronger.

(3) 排演课本剧。

课本剧是学生在教师指导下，通过表演形象地呈现语言材料的一种方法。它以教室为舞台，由学生扮演不同的角色。课本剧的使用弥补了语言环境的不足，拓宽了学生用外语思维的空间，深受小学生的喜爱。

案例

英语剧本： A Proud Peacock（骄傲的孔雀）

小松鼠：（软翻上）

小猴：（围着小松鼠）Great! Let me have a try.

狐狸：（追上）Hi! You two，don't play any more. The forest concert is going to begin. You'd better go and prepare for it.

小猴：Look，I'm just preparing for it.

狐狸：You naught monkey! Don't play any more.

小松鼠：Let's go! Little monkey!

小猴：Would you like to go with us，Fox?

狐狸：Thanks! But I'm going to invite the peacock to our concert.

I'll be back soon.

狐狸：See you later!

（自言自语地）My beautiful peacock. Where are you? Can you hear me?（狐狸下）

孔雀（上）：Hi，I'm a peacock! Look! How pretty I am! My colorful feathers.

My beautiful cockscomb. Who have these just like mine?

Oh! What are you saying?

Have I got any friends? Oh, no, no. I don't need any friends. My only friend is me.

狐狸（上）：Hello! My beautiful peacock. I'm looking for you everywhere.

孔雀：Looking for me?

狐狸：Oh, yes! We are holding a forest concert.

Would you like to join us?

孔雀：Oh, no, no. I never play with any ugly ones.

Look! Your ears are so long.

They are too terrible. And all of your friends are ugly too. Do you think so?（对观众）

狐狸：My beautiful peacock. You are too proud.

That's bad for you. Although we are not beautiful.

We'll help you when necessary. Please be our friend. And please take part in our concert. We all like your dance.

孔雀：Oh, no, no. I never dance for any ugly ones. And I'll never need your helps.

狐狸：My beautiful peacock…

孔雀：（打断狐狸的话）Don't say any more. You ugly fox.

狐狸：Oh, I have to leave now. You are too proud.

孔雀：（独白）Oh, what a lovely day. The sun is shining brightly.

Why not have a good sleep under this tall tree?

大灰狼：（自言自语）I'm so hungry. I'm so hungry.

Those elves are staying together.

I hear they are having a forest concert today.

I have no chance to catch them. I'm so hungry. Oh, there's a big hole in the tree.

What's in it? Is there something for me?

Oh, what's that? A beautiful peacock.

I think I won't be hungry any longer. Look! The two fat arms. They are delicious.

孔雀：（惊吓的）Oh! My god. Who's that? What are you doing for?

大灰狼：Aha! I'm your good friend. Don't be afraid.

孔雀：I haven't got any friends.

大灰狼：That's OK! Otherwise I'll have no such a chance.

孔雀：You, you are a wolf. You evil one.

大灰狼：You are right. I'm so hungry. And you are my good dinner.

孔雀：Help! Help!

大灰狼：Don't run away. My little dear!

猴子：（出）Listen! Someone is shouting help!

狐狸、松鼠：（跑上）Who is crying for help?

（幕内）孔雀：Help! Help! A big wolf is going to kill me!

松鼠：Perhaps it's the peacock.

猴子：Oh, my god! A wolf is running after her. My friends.

Let's go and help her quickly.

狐狸：Let me ask Brother Dear to come. Brother Dear! Brother Dear!

孔雀：Help! Help!（声音渐弱）

鹿：（出）Stop! Stop! You evil one!

猴子、松鼠：Stop! Stop! You evil one!

大灰狼：Get away! You! Get away! Or I'll kill you.

鹿：If you don't want to die, You'd better leave here right now.

大灰狼：Forgive me! Forgive me!

鹿：Don't bully us again.

大灰狼：I won't! I won't!

孔雀：Thank you ! Thank you very much. I would have die but for you!

猴子：Don't cry any more!

鹿：Let me have a look at your wound. Nothing serious!

My beautiful peacock! Let me help you!

孔雀：Thanks a lot! Let me be your friend. Let me give you my beautiful dance.

众：Welcome! Welcome!

鹿：Now let's go and have our forest concert.

众：Ok! Let's go together!

6. 给学生提供有趣味性的朗读材料

学生对贴近生活、有趣味性且与其水平相当的朗读材料才会产生兴趣，因此对于朗读材料的选择，应多选择一些有情节的小故事、朗朗上口的英语童谣儿歌和一些绕口令。如对高年级学生，教师可提供《英语角·英文小读者》，那里面有许多学生感兴趣的故事、儿歌，同时还可以鼓励学生去投稿。对低年级学生，教师可以鼓励他们去看《爱冒险的朵拉》，有条件的学生可以买下《爱冒险的朵拉》书学习英语。学生非常喜欢这些英语书籍，教师还可利用上课时间给他们展示的机会，让他们朗读故事或表演关于朵拉的片段。

教师在培养学生英语朗读能力的同时，要注意自身英语朗读水平的提高，学生对英语语音的感性认识绝大部分来自对教师的模仿。如果教师的英语朗读不地道，学生的朗读必定会受影响，如果教师的朗读没有感情、没有节奏，要求小学生有感情、有节奏地朗读是不现实的。

（三）阅读

阅读是儿童学习、认识周围世界的主要途径，可以丰富知识、促进智力，并获得情感、社会性等方面的发展。阅读可以提高学生语言的输入量，提高学生的语言表达能力，为今后的说打下一个良好的基础。

阅读的操练应该通过循序渐进的方法来进行，通常分为阅读前、阅读中、阅读后三个阶段。

1. 阅读前

阅读前先要复习相关的单词和交际用语；接着应初步学习要涉及的新的语言项目；最后通过某种方式使学生大概知道阅读材料的大意，或者是设置悬念，引起学生阅读的兴趣。

读前活动不宜过多，它的作用是营造学习氛围，调动学习兴趣，激活相关知识，把学生带入阅读的文章中，而不是匆匆忙忙地把学生赶入阅读文章，在学生没有准备好的情况下，强迫学生阅读。

2. 阅读中

可以先让学生个人或分成小组阅读，朗读或默读都可以；接着进一步处理新的语言项目，如单词等，在处理单词的时候可以与阅读理解同步；然后设计相应的阅读理解练习，如回答问题、判断对错等。最后大声朗读阅读材料。

在阅读中，教师要明确学生阅读的困难是什么，是背景知识、语言知识还是阅读方法。教师要选择影响学生理解文本的新词或文化背景知识进行讲解或补充，并培养学生用猜测的方法去猜测词义，以及克服稍微遇到点困难就畏缩不前的不自信心理。

阅读中的重点是让学生在读的过程中理解关键内容，获得关键信息。所以教师可以在读的过程中让学生“做一些事情”，比如把打乱的句子重新排列顺序，构成一篇逻辑合理的文章，并仔细阅读找到问题的答案。这种做做读读的活动是小学生感兴趣的方式。因为基于游戏的阅读更能激发学生阅读的兴趣和胆量，他们会读得更主动，思维会更活跃。

3. 阅读后

读后活动最好和读的内容有所联系，要贴近学生的生活实际。教师在阅读的环节要强调语言的运用。

案例

人教版《英语》（PEP 版）第十册 Lesson 64

Wonderful Food

Food, food, wonderful food. We need many kinds of food to be healthy. Look at the food pyramid. It shows us what we should eat every day. We should eat a lot of food from the bottom of the pyramid. We should eat plenty of fruit and vegetables. We need some chicken, fish or meat, and we need some milk or yogurt. We should eat only a little from the top of the pyramid. We only need a little fat and sugar. Remember, we shouldn't eat too much junk food.

阅读前：

(1) 教师通过 Brain Storming（头脑风暴游戏）的形式让学生分两组进行比赛，复习学过的有关 fruit，vegetable，food 的食物词汇，目的是激活学生头脑里已有的知识，为本课所学知识做铺垫。

(2) 教师让学生对最喜爱的食物的问卷结果展开讨论，目的是激发兴趣，拉近文本与学生之间的距离。

(3) 教师对学生可能遇到的新词进行讲解，目的是提前解决理解困难。教师先通过讨论造句的方式帮助学生理解 energy。What can we do with energy? We can swim/play basketball…接着让学生观看图片，用分音节朗读的方式讲授 pyramid，用图片对比方式帮助学生理解 a little，some，plenty of，a lot of 等词。

(4) 和学生一起了解食物金字塔的外形，目的是提前感知文本，为阅读活动打下基础。

阅读中：

阅读中的主要任务是帮助学生形成积极有效的阅读策略。教师设计的主要活动是填写“食物金字塔”。这是学生参与活动的兴趣点，它能帮助学生准确把握文章的核心内容。通过填写“食物金字塔”，学生了解了金字塔的最底层应该由 noodles，rice，dumpling，bread 和其他谷物类食品（other cereals）构成，第二层由 vegetables，fruit 构成，第三层由 chicken，fish，meat，milk，yogurt 构成，第四层（顶层）由 hamburger，pizza，ice-cream，candies 构成。学生能够表达 We should eat a lot of noodles，rice，dumplings and bread. We should eat plenty of vegetables and fruit. We should eat some chicken，fish，meat，milk and yogurt. We should eat a little hamburger，pizza，ice-cream and candies.

另外，填写“食物金字塔”也能帮助教师了解学生阅读理解的程度，让学生及时反馈在阅读活动中遇到的困难。将文本内容“图形化”，其表达的内容更直观，这样便于将复述文章大意的活动“大众化”。学生完成金字塔，也为读后交际活动做了铺垫。

阅读后：

教师设计了 3 个活动：

(1) 请学生提出健康饮食的建议。教师把调查表再次给学生看，请学生用 should，shouldn't 提建议。

(2) 让学生回忆本课所学，教师根据学生回答进行梳理，教师可以给出新的语言支撑点，如 I like…My favorite food is…Now I see…I should…I shouldn't…这样做的好处是帮助复习巩固，并使知识系统化。

(3) 让学生提出更多的保持健康的建议，问学生除了健康饮食外，还有什么其他方式可以保持健康，如运动、保持好心情等。其目的是激活旧知识，达到其与新知识的融合。

二、读的游戏

教师要抓住小学生争强好胜、爱表演的特点，积极运用读的游戏使小学生保持对读的持续兴趣。

1. 抽卡片读单词（Choose the card）

游戏说明：抽到国王或王后可以不读，抽到其他卡片，上面写着数字几就读几遍。

2. 眼神暗示（Look and say）

游戏说明：在读单词时，老师的眼神看着谁，谁就要读单词。或者老师轻轻说出学生的名字，听到自己名字的学生就要读单词。这个游戏可以让学生上课注意听讲。

3. 夹句型（Choose the sentences）

游戏说明：教师将今天所有的句型写在一条条的白纸上并放入一个桶里，请学生用筷子将句型条夹出来，当夹出句型条时学生可以用手将纸打开并将句型读出来，可以让两个小组进行比赛，最快读出来的那组获胜。

4. 小白兔回家（Go home）

游戏说明：用于操练已学单词。老师将所学单词写在卡片上，一张一张展示，每次展示时，第一个读出来单词的学生可以向前走一步，看谁先回到“家”。

5. 钓鱼（Catch fish）

游戏说明：在鱼图案后面分别贴上哭脸和笑脸。鱼身上写上单词号，钓到哪条鱼就读相应的单词，如果是笑脸可以抽奖。如果是哭脸，则把所有的单词都读一遍。

6. 转盘（Spinner）

游戏说明：老师制作一个转盘，在转盘的最外圈贴上所学单词，让学生转动转盘，转到哪一个单词就读哪一个单词，转到 Sticker 就得 Sticker。

7. 空中拦截（Stand on the newspaper）

游戏说明：分两组。准备两张报纸。每组各出一个人站在铺开的报纸上，抢读单词。不正确或是速度慢的同学脚下的报纸就会被对折，直到脚触地板，脚触地板者为输者。

8. 抢椅子（Get the chair）

游戏说明：老师在教室前面摆三个椅子，叫四个学生到前面来，然后老师和学生一起读已学单词或句子，当老师停下来的时候学生就要去抢椅子，没抢到椅子的学生就要被罚读一个单词，然后回去。

9. 设陷阱（Set a trap）

游戏说明：让学生跟读卡片上的单词，老师故意经常读错，读对时学生可以跟读，读错时学生必须马上做出反应，双手叉腰，瞪着眼睛，做出生气的样子，但不准发出任何声音。反应错误的淘汰，也可采取小组记分。

10. 踩地雷（Bomb）

游戏说明：选定一个单词为地雷，老师领读很多个单词，读到该单词的时候，有谁跟着读了，就是中地雷了，其他学生就一起指着他说："one，two，three，bomb."

第四节　写的操练

写的过程是从内部语言到外部语言的转换，也就是表达和复用的过程。领会和吸收是基础，表达和复用是提高。

小学英语教学中的写是指书写和写作。书写包括字母、由字母组成的单词，以及由标点和单词组成的句子。书写若不规范、字迹潦草或错误百出，必然使人看不清或读不懂，令人生厌；反之，美观流畅的书写会给人以美的享受。写作是学生用英语表达自己思想和情感的过程，也是用英文影响别人的过程。在写的操练中，要注意培养学生做到语句通顺、语法规范、内容完整、详略得当。

一、写的形式

（一）书写

课堂30分钟后，学生们完成了紧张的学习任务，听、说、读等活动已经让学生们显得很疲劳。此时，适当的书写训练会让整节课动静结合，让学生有效地达到语言的输出。在书写训练上，教师应避免过于强调接受性学习、单纯机械模仿、死记硬背、机械训练的教学方法。具体可采取以下方法：

1. 传统的写

教师要告诉学生书写的八字原则："重合、充满格、有斜度。"教师一定要示范到位，让学生模仿，并及时纠正他们的书写。教师事先要讲好要求，如作业纸的大小、书写格式、笔的类型等，要求学生在5分钟之内把单词书写5遍，每个单词写一个汉语意思及音标，下课铃响，组长收作业，一般能收到98%的作业，教师批改后及时反馈。

2. 变形抄写

小学阶段，让学生来默写单词是一件比较困难的事，学生厌倦，出错率高，影响了学生学习英语的积极性。因此教师在教学中让学生默写的次数应远远少于抄写。抄写不能局限于简单的机械抄写，教师要变换方法，激发学生的书写兴趣。教师可以让学生自己归类单词并利用小笔记来积累归类好的单词；让学生翻开书找要求写的某些单词，比速度，训练学生的单词记忆，并增加学生看单词表的次数。抄写单词的形式有：某一类的词（如水果）、单词接龙、只写四个字母的单词、写含有 a 等字母的单词。

3. 充分展示

通过一定的训练，学生的书写能力大大提高了。但日常书写满足不了学生的个性需求。因此，教师可以举办竞赛等活动，把学生的书写能力尽情展示出来。如学生作品在评选后可作为班级墙报的一部分；举办小型的“书法小能手”比赛，让学生在规定时间内完成书写内容，按时间排序，写错者淘汰，取前十名的学生奖励；也可利用校内英语节等活动，举办丰富多彩的书写比赛，如卡通字母秀、SUPER 词霸、手抄报大比拼等活动。总之，要让学生们充分展示自己的英语水平，调动他们书写的积极性。英语书写是一项重要的基本功，对于提高学生的文化素质起着重要作用，应从起始年级就严格要求、严格训练。要逐步培养学生的书写能力，直到学生养成良好的学习习惯为止。

(二) 写作

1. 造句

造句是英语写作教学的主要练习形式之一。教师可以从扩词开始。如 bike 一词，可让学生扩充成 a bike—a black bike—a small black bike—a new small black bike；student 一词扩展为 a student—a boy student—a tall boy student—a good tall boy student。接着，做一些造句练习。如用 Tom 一词造句，答案有 Tom is a boy. Tom isn't Chinese. How old is Tom? Is Tom a student? That's Tom's mother. Does Tom have any English books? Where is Tom from? 然后，教师可选用一些替换练习。如：

T：She is eleven.（He/You/I/Mary）

S：He is eleven. You are eleven. I am eleven. Mary is eleven.

还可就表语部分进行替换。

教师在让学生造句时可以提供一个结合实际生活的情境，避免因注重语言形式而忽视内容，脱离一定的情境与主题。如在学了“My Favorite food”单元后，让学生学习造句：“I like fish. It's fresh. It's my favorite.”“The potatoes are salty，they're tasty and yummy.”

2. 句型转换

在操练中要注重对学生进行句型转换的操练，让学生在不改变语言意义的前提下进行句型转换练习，理解表达同一个意思可以采用不同的句型，以免出现写作时句型单调重复。

案例 1

用同义词或同义词组对原句中的某些词或词组进行替换，注意转换后的词或词组的词形要与句子其他成分相适应。

(1) That day we could see flowers here and there.

That day we could see flowers ____________.

(everywhere)

(2) The teacher always takes good care of the children in the school.

The teacher always ________ ________ the children in the school.

(looks after)

(3) Mr. Smith is working.

Mr. Smith is ________ ________.

(at work)

案例2

运用反义词（组）的否定式进行转换。

(1) It's clear that this visit is different from last time.

It's clear that this visit is not the ________ ________ last time.

(same as)

(2) I think wealth is less important than health.

I ________ think wealth is ________ important than health.

(don't, more)

(3) The runner couldn't catch up with others in the race.

The runner ________ ________ others in the race.

(fell behind)

案例3

运用主动语态与被动语态的变化来转换同义词，注意时态、动词的一致性。

(1) Everyone should give back the library books on time.

Library books should ________ ________ ________ on time.

(be given back)

(2) It is widely accepted that more people use computers in the world today.

Computers ________ widely ________ in the world today.

(are, used)

(3) The farm grows cotton.

Cotton ________ ________ ________ ________ ________.

(is grown on the farm)

案例 4

非延续性动词与延续性动词的转换。

(1) The manager left two hours ago.

The manager ________ ________ ________ for two hours.

(has been away)

(2) The film began five minutes ago.

The film has been ________ ________ five minutes.

(on for)

(3) Mr. Li joined the Party twenty years ago.

Mr. Li ________ ________ ________ the Party for twenty years.

(has been in)

案例 5

将直接引语变为间接引语，或将间接引语转换成直接引语。

(1) "I've found my wallet," he said to me.

He ________ me that he ________ ________ the wallet.

(told, had found)

(2) "Did you see her last week?" he said.

He ________ ________ I had seen her the week ________.

(asked, if/weather, before)

案例 6

将简单句变成同义的复合句，或将复合句变成同义的简单句。

(1) We didn't go out for a walk because it was raining.

We didn't go out for a walk ________ ________ the rain.

(because of)

(2) He was so excited that he couldn't go to sleep.

He was ________ ________ ________ go to sleep.

(too excited to)

(3) You should put them back after you use them.

You should put them back ________ ________ them.

(after using)

案例 7

将并列句变成同义的复合句，或将复合句变成同义的并列句。

（1）Come on，or we will miss the early bus.

________ we ________ hurry，we will miss the early bus.

（If，don't）

（2）The man gave us a talk last week. Now he will give us another talk this week.

The man ________ gave us a talk last week ________ ________ another talk this week.

（who，will give us）

案例 8

运用关联连词连接或合并句子。

（1）Tom can't speak Japanese well and Jim can't，either.

________ Tom ________ Jim can speak Japanese well.

（Neither，nor）

（2）Jean has read the book and Alice has read it，too.

________ Jean ________ Alice have read the book.

（Both，and）

（3）This store sells man's clothes，and it also sells woman's clothes.

This store sells ________ ________ man's clothes ________ ________ woman's clothes.

（not only，but also）

案例 9

用 it 作形式主语的句型进行转换。

（1）He can finish the work easily.

________ ________ ________ for him to finish the work.

（It is easy）

（2）To learn English well is not easy.

It is not easy ________ ________ English well.

（to learn）

3. 小练笔

人教版《英语》（PEP 版）为学生们进行创作提供了强有力的保障。它所蕴含的丰富资源让教师可以用一种全新的理念、个性化的操练来引导学生们掌握新知识。教师要把课本上的内容加以延伸和扩展，模仿课文的主题，引入实际生活让学生写小练笔。如五年级上册第一单元是介绍新老师，学完新知识后，教师在操练环节可以让学生模仿课文综合运用所学知识描写自己的家庭和生活情况。学生的创作欲望和积极性很高。

案例 1

来看一位学生的小练笔

My Family

Hi! I'm John. I am ten years old. I live in New Century Garden near school. I go to school every day. In my family there are three people. My father，my mother and I. My father is a doctor. He is kind and friendly. He has a lot of friends. He likes computer very much. My mother is a business woman. She likes watching TV very much. She does housework every day. I love my family.

还有一位学生描写一次乡下的经历，短文充满好奇、新鲜感：

Saturday　　May 25th，2013　　Hot

My father，my mother and I went to the countryside by car. My grandma was ill，and we visited her. I played with my cousin. We went to the field to catch butterflies. I saw real pigs for the first time. They ran away when they saw us. Pigs are very lovely. They are fat.

学生们一篇篇稚嫩的小创作，构成了一个绚丽多彩的万花筒。在操练的过程中，他们像小精灵一样，向我们描绘了一个个色彩斑斓的、充满童话的世界。

案例 2

周末活动小练笔

(1) 去公园休闲。

时间：Saturday/Sunday morning/afternoon

地点：garden

人物：Jack and I（可替换）

事件：paint，boating，climb，take photos，play games（可替换）

学生的小练笔：

Today is Sunday. It's a sunny day. The sky is so blue. Jack and I go to the garden for fun. The lake is very clear. And there are many people boating on the lake. The flowers are blooming and the trees are green. Jack play guitar and I sing. We talk and sing. We all have a good time. How I wish we can come again!

(2) 去购物。

时间：Saturday/Sunday morning/afternoon

地点：street

人物：Jack，Mary and I（可替换）

事件：go shopping（可替换）

学生的小练笔：

Today is Saturday. It's cloudy. We are so excited because today is Mary's birthday. Jack and I go to the street to buy a gift for Mary. There are many people, a lot of shops and nice things in the street. We choose some flowers for her. We wish Mary have a good time and happy birthday.

（3）去运动。

时间：Saturday/Sunday morning/afternoon

地点：playground

人物：Jack and I（可替换）

事件：play basketball，football（可替换）

学生的小练笔：

Today is Sunday. It's sunny. The sky is so blue and the air is fresh. We have no lessons. Jack and I go to the playground for fun. We play basketball. It's very interesting. We are tired but we have a good time. How I wish we can play again.

还有一位学生以操场所见来写：

Today is Sunday. It's sunny. The sky is so blue and the air is fresh. We have no lessons. Jack and I go out to have a walk. The birds are singing in the trees，the flowers are beautiful. We walk and talk. We meet many people. Some people are talking，some are listening to music，others are walking the dogs. We are all very happy.

4. 看图写话

案例

先看图说话，以旧带新，引出并学习 go sightseeing，make snowman，sit by the fire 等。

go sightseeing
play in the park
plant trees

swim　eat ice-cream
wear shorts and skirt
go on holiday

pick the fruit
go sightseeing
fly kite

ski
make snowman
sit by the fire

然后让学生试着看图写话，要求如下：

Now let's write something about your favorite season（练习运用所学句型描述自己喜爱的季节）

First，you must tell the people what's your favorite season.

Second，you can talk about how the season is.

Third，you can tell the people why you like the season.

Give the model.

Model

My Favorite Season

My favorite season is winter. The weather in winter is very cold. The temperature is below 10℃. It often snows. The people often sit by the fire and watch TV at home. Some people go skiing or make snowmen outside. I like winter best. Because I like skiing. And I can make snowmen with my friends.

5. "交互式"写作

英语课程标准要求学生能以小组讨论的方式起草和修改作文，能与他人合作，共同完成学习任务。约翰斯认为写作不完全是个人行为，而是发生在团体之中的行为，因此他提倡用交互式（interactive）的方法训练写作。所谓交互主要是指作者和读者之间相互的作用，因为从某种意义上说，作品往往是作者和读者共同合作完成的。英语课程标准在技能教学参考表中要求学生能够相互修改，个人或小组面批，检查语言、文法、逻辑、用词等方面的内容。

写作不能仅仅理解成个人的行为，因此在操练中不宜总是采取单独写出作文来让教师批改的模式，而应该提倡学生开展两人或数人小组活动，通过讨论合作完成写作。操练结束后，教师应大声朗读学生的作品，这样既可以激发写的动机与兴趣，又可营造轻松愉快的气氛，使得写的过程有读者参与，作者和读者彼此交流，互相学习。

在“交互式”写作的操练中，有效利用交互式电子白板（interactive whiteboard）往往能收到很好的效果。交互式电子白板在国外出现得相对较早，并得到了政府的支持。其中，以英国最为突出。英国政府先后于2003年、2004年为交互式电子白板投入了共2 500万英镑。

交互式电子白板在写的操练环节能增强学生对教学内容的理解和掌握，增强写的操练的创造性和交互性，有利于知识的消化。

案例1

在学习了Christmas这一单元后，学生初步了解了关于节日的一些表达方法，也了解了西方人过节时的礼仪和习俗。根据教学大纲，教师安排了“辨一辨，连一连，想一想，填一填”的教学内容，并要求学生写一篇关于中西方节日对比的作文。

教学过程设计：

(1) 创设情境，初步感知。

T：Boys and girls，we have learned about the Christmas，and there are a lot of interesting things on that day. Do you remember?

S：Yes.

T：Good. But as we all know，we Chinese have the similar day like Americans that is Spring Festival. Today we will learn to write about the similarities and the differences between the American new year “Christmas” and the Chinese new year “Spring Festival”.

First，let's look at two videos. Please look at them carefully and then we will do some exercises.

(利用交互式电子白板播放视频。)

(2) 讨论交流，激发灵感。

T：OK，that's all. What can you see in the two videos? Can you remember? Now let's talk about the similarities and the differences between the two festivals. You can discuss in groups.

T：(随时观察讨论情况，适时给予帮助。)

T：Ok，boys and girls. Please stop here. I know that you all learn the points. Here are the things you have just seen in the videos. Now let's finish some tasks. I will show the pictures and you will speak out which it belongs to，the Christmas or the Spring Festival?

(教师切换交互式电子白板画面，向学生展示任务。根据视频及课本内容，教师利用交互式电子白板的聚光灯功能逐一展示事物，请学生回答。教师要及时给予反馈。)

T：(进行总结) You are very clever. Now I would like to choose some of you to link the things on the whiteboard，to “China” or to “America”.

（教师切换界面，交互式电子白板上出现不同的事物，如不同的食物、圣诞树、圣诞卡片、压岁钱等。教师让学生通过连线的方法归类，并邀请2～3位同学到交互式电子白板前，利用画笔功能进行连线。）

T：Ok，all of you have done a very good job. Now，Let's think. What else can we do on Christmas or Spring Festival?

S：（学生思考并回答。）

T：Ok，let's fill the blanks together and finish these sentences.

（教师切换界面，交互式电子白板上呈现出不完整的句子。学生上前填入不同的词语和句子。）

Before Christmas，we ____________. /When Spring Festival is coming，we eat ____________，put on ____________，play ____________ and ____________. （利用交互式电子白板荧光笔可选择颜色的功能，让学生填写的部分呈现红色，更加醒目。）

该环节可以考查学生是否掌握了写作内容要领。"想一想"是为了让学生拓宽思路，不拘泥于课本和视频。"填一填"是为了让学生回忆有关节日的表达方式，为以后的成文做准备。

案例2

使学生从不同的角度对一篇习作进行较为合理的点评。

教学过程设计：

(1) 展示习作，教师引导。

T：Boys and girls. We have learned how to describe seasons，and yesterday I told you to write a passage about your favorite season. You all have finished very well. I know that you all have tried your best. Now，let's look at your works.

（教师利用交互式电子白板呈现范文，并同时使用其遮幕功能，先呈现学生甲的作文，后呈现学生乙的作文。注：学生乙的作文要略优于学生甲的。）

学生甲……　　　　　　学生乙……

T：I will show you one by one and let's think about whose is better and who is the Star of this time?

（范文的展示唤起了作文作者的记忆，也使得其他学生充满了好奇。）

(2) 比一比，帮一帮。

T：Now I want you to talk about the following writings in groups and give me your points. Which part is good and which part is not that good and why. Finally，speak out your methods to improve it.

（学生分小组热烈讨论并回答。教师根据学生的不同回答，在交互白板上选择不同颜色荧光笔做出标记；对于写得好的部分，教师则用交互式电子白板的放大功能进行放大，让学生更清晰地看到。）

T：（教师总结）I'm so glad that your statements are well-done. Can you sum up your ideas into several aspects?

（教师举例示范）

S：（按照教师的引导，从单词的拼写、语法、作文内容等方面进行评价。）

T：Now I want to invite the author to say something about his writing.

S：（发言）

T：（总结学生的发言，进行补充，并将补充的内容以板书的形式呈现在交互式电子白板上，让学生直观地感知对他人作品进行评价的思路和方法，同时学会在英语作文中抒发自己的感情。）

二、写的游戏

写的游戏有助于培养小学生良好的书写习惯和书写规范。

1. 火眼金睛（Eyes and ears）

游戏说明：教师只摆口形，不出声音。学生要根据老师的口型写单词或句子。

2. 身体字母（Body letters）

游戏说明：准备计时器，比赛时将学生分组，让他们在规定时间内用身体组合将 26 个字母表演出来，可以一人演，也可以几人组合演。老师在一旁当裁判。将每组表演出来的字母写在黑板上，看哪组在规定的时间内表演的字母更多。

3. 看图写单词（Look and write）

游戏说明：教师事先把需操练的 20 个单词写在小黑板上或白纸上，先不要让学生们看见，然后将全班按四人一组分成若干小组。竞赛开始，教师将小黑板或白纸挂起来，让学生们看一分钟，然后收起来，再给学生们两分钟时间将看到的单词写出来，写得最多最正确的组获胜。

4. 画一条线（Draw a line）

游戏说明：教师在黑板上写一个要操练的单词，每一次只写一个字母，学生猜教师在写什么，第一个猜对的学生在黑板上写下一个单词。

5. 谜语（Riddles）

游戏说明：教师拿出装满谜语的盒子，学生们以男女生对抗的形式，轮流随意从盒子里选择一张进行猜测，然后写下答案，写得又快又对的获胜。

如 This is a person. When you are sick, you will go to see him. He always wears white uniform. He will check your body and give you some medicine. He can help you get well. Who is he? A doctor.（画线部分为答案）

6. 找朋友（What's missing?）

游戏说明：先让学生“认一认、读一读”（单词随着背景音乐不断变换），然后完成下表，又快又对者获胜。

7. 讲故事（Telling tales）

游戏说明：在黑板上写出三个单词，第一个是人物，第二个是地点，第三个是表示事件的动词。比如“The Queen”“beach”“skipping”。让学生发挥自己的想象力来编写小故事。写完后，读给同桌听，并请同桌纠正文中的语法错误，然后每两人中选一个大声读出自己的小故事，其他同学和老师边听边纠正其文中的语法错误。

老师在给出单词时越随意，编出的小故事就越有意思，故事越离奇越能引起学生的兴趣。

8. 拼写比赛会（Spelling bee）

游戏说明：教师在黑板上写出一个比较长的单词，把全班学生分成 2～3 组，要求各组低声讨论用单词中的任何一个字母来造一个以该字母开头的已学过的单词，在限定的时间内写出单词最多的组为获胜者，获胜组选一个学生大声拼出所写单词，其他组静听。如：

dictionary

A 组	B 组
desk	dog
ice	red
rat	ink
cook	cat
…	…

9. 问答一连串（A chain of asking and answering）

游戏说明：每个学生准备一张练习纸，在纸的顶头随意写上一个问题，然后传给下一个同学；第二个同学将问题的答案写在纸上，并添加一个新的问题，然后再传给第三个同学，以此类推。如：

Student 1：What are you going to do after the lesson?

Student 2：I am going to go back home. What's the weather like?

Student 3：It's cold today. What kind of sports activities do you like?

……

在传递5～6次之后，请一位同学把前面的问题和答案大声朗读出来。此游戏可采用pair work或group work来做。

第六章

应用环节的设计

本章导读

应用环节是在操练的基础上放松控制，让学生综合地运用所学的语言知识，把单项的语言技能提高为运用语言交换信息的能力。这一环节可以借助表演、游戏、复述等手段，目的是让学生能够达到举一反三、活学活用的水平，最大限度地运用所学的语言知识去进行交际。

第一节 表 演

表演不仅是一种结果、一次演出，更是一个学习的过程。它能使学生在实践中巩固新知识，促使学生开口说英语，并帮助学生在语言有限的情况下，利用身体语言、面部表情等非语言表达形式进行交流，使语言更真实、更有意义、更易于记忆。

一、对话表演

英语对话表演对帮助学生牢固记忆对话内容、培养学生的英语学习兴趣有很大作用。它能有效地排除学生怕开口说英语的心理障碍，充分挖掘学生的学习潜能。

1. 对话表演要注重逼真性、丰富性

国外的实验证明：形象越具体、越鲜明、越活泼、越新颖，就越能缩短感知时间，也就越能激发学生认知和活动的兴趣，越能提高教学效率。小学生的对话表演并非出自真心真意，他们只是在从众心理的驱使下，机械地进行着对话。对仅凭兴趣来决定喜好，思维在很大程度上还依靠直观的、具体的内容，受外界影响很大的小学生来说，教师要努力创设近似于真实的表演环境。为对话表演布置有趣的装饰，编排适当的甚至夸张的情节等均有助于产生肺腑之“演”的效果。

案例 1

以人教版《英语》（PEP 版）四年级上册 Unit 6 Meet My Family 的内容为例，教师在教授完对话后将教室布置成了“家”：在讲台上放了一把椅子作为客厅，在讲台下放了一把椅子作为孩子的卧室，安排两名同学 A 与 B，A 坐在讲台下的椅子上玩，B 扮演“喜羊羊”，到教室门外去告诉全班同学，他要到 A 同学家做客。A 在向喜羊羊介绍他的家人时，要请同学们努力配合，如 A 指着谁说：“This is my mother.”这位同学就要做出妈妈的样子，起身和喜羊羊握手问好。运用英语相互介绍的表演由此展开，这些生活化的环境创设，可以大大调动学生参与表演的积极性，既让学生掌握了介绍方法，也让学生学习了如何尊重对方。

案例 2

给表演的角色戴上一个与其形象身份相符的头饰，直观的刺激有利于学生认识角色、理解角色，也有利于学生进入角色。如在学习了“Who are you?”“Nice/Glad to meet you.”以及一些动物名称之后，教师可以让学生们戴着动物头饰进行自我介绍并相互问好。

S1：Hello! I'm Deer. Who are you?

S2：Hello! I'm Tiger.

S1：Nice to meet you.

S2：Nice to meet you，too.

头饰使原本单调的对话变得生动活泼，头饰在学生之间架起了英语交流的桥梁，促进了语言的交流与运用。

案例 3

以人教版《英语》（PEP 版）四年级上册 Unit 3 My Friends 的内容为例，教师可以在对话表演的情节编排上动脑筋。设计“神探柯南”的游戏，首先让两位学生扮演警察，另外四五个学生当过路人，教师借助多媒体播放：一名少年骑自行车撞到了一位老奶奶，老奶奶伤得很重，但是肇事者逃离了现场。请目击者（过路人）协助警察调查，描述这位少年的外貌，找到这位少年。同学们表现欲望强烈，争相运用所学句型：He is a man. He has short black hair and small eyes. He has a big nose and a small mouth…全班气氛热烈，不仅复习巩固了所学知识，还培养了学生助人为乐的精神。

2. 对话表演形式要灵活多变

一些学者认为：要培养学习者的交际能力，最有效的办法之一就是把学习者置于具体的交际场合中去，让学习者使用所学的语言来满足他的实际需求。因此，丰富对话表演中的“对话”形式，不失为提高学生语言运用能力的有效方法。

案例 1

一位教师第一次给学生示范“Rain”的表演时，只是使用拟人手法，将自己化身为“Rain”，作自我介绍：“I'm the rain. I'm coming…”学生们仿照老师顺利进行了表演，教学效果一般。但课后，教研组长给了她建议：如果在名词前加上修饰词，再加上雨声，则更有感染力，学生的表演欲会更强烈，表演效果也会更好。于是，这位教师将表演的语言改为：“I'm the happy rain. I'm coming，pitter-patter，pitter-patter.”结果学生们被调动起来，他们争先恐后地表演起来。有的学生说：“I'm the big rain. I'm coming. Hua-Lala，Hua-Lala.”有的学生说：“I'm the little rain. I'm coming. Di-da，di-da.”还有的说：“I'm the rain. I can fly! I'm coming.”

案例 2

引导学生在竞争、抗衡中培养竞争意识，锻炼语言能力。以人教版《英语》(PEP 版)三年级下册 Unit 1 Welcome Back to School 的内容为例，教师可设计表演活动：给每组发一面国旗，每个组分别代表相应的国家。当教师出示国旗并问：“Where are you from?”代表相应国家的一组马上站起来回答：“We are from…”中间有快速反应游戏：教师手里拿着两张单词卡片（boy，girl）。当教师出示单词 boy 时，男同学站起来；当教师出示单词 girl 时，女同学站起来，看谁反应快，反应慢的淘汰出局。还有猜图片的游戏：教师在屏幕上呈现 8 个人物，即花园宝宝的朋友们。他们的脸被遮盖了，教师要求学生根据部分图片猜测是 boy 还是 girl。结束阶段有 Costume Party：让学生穿戴好事先准备的化装舞会要用的服装，然后以组为单位上来表演。当一些同学表演时，其他同学要带着任务猜“He is a boy. She is a girl”。丰富的活动使同学们饶有兴趣地参与其中，既锻炼了语言运用能力，也培养了集体荣誉感和团队合作能力。

本杰明·富兰克林说：“告诉我，我就忘了；教我，我就记住了；让我参与，我就学会了。”在对话表演中，教师要充分把握学生的实际特点，创设逼真、丰富的情境，引导学生积极参与和主动投入，让学生从“要我演”变成“我要演”“我会演”“我善演”。

二、故事表演

对于小学生来说，故事有很大的吸引力，儿童的生活环境和活动范围相对狭小，他们对世界有着强烈的探索欲望，故事提供的虚拟世界突破了平淡而狭小的现实世界，故事跨越了时空的界限，为儿童的想象提供了空间和机会，能唤起学生强烈的情绪反应，增强学生的记忆。

故事的选择要贴近实际，要根据学生的具体情况和教材特点选择故事，并进行适当的改编。如果剧本太难，学生会因为难度太大而失去信心。故事演练时要注意合理安排角色，不能随意安排，要给学生安排适合他们自己的角色，使他们能更加投入进去。在表演中，对于学生出现的错误不要马上纠正，找个适当的时候告诉他们或是让同学们自己找错误，不能打击他们的积极性。教师只是帮手、导演，学生才是真正的主角。

案例 1

步骤 1　提供故事

故事素材：

The Magic Picture

Mr. White is an old English teacher. He comes from London. He is teaching English in our school.

One day, he comes into the classroom and puts a simple drawing on the wall.

He says to us, "Look at my picture here. It is a magic one." There is only a little boy in the picture. Why is it a magic picture? No one knows.

Mr. White says to the little boy, "Could you tell me your name please?"

The little boy in the picture smiles and says, "Yes, sir. My name is Paul. I'm glad to see you, sir."

The children in our class are excited! "What a magic picture! The boy can speak English! His name is Paul!"

After class, Lanlan, Lily, Li Gang, Liu Lei and I stand in front of the picture. We want to make Paul speak English. "Speak English!" Lanlan says. No answer. "Look at me and tell me your name!" Li Gang says. No answer. Liu Lei shouts to Paul, "You bad boy! Tell us your name!" Still no answer.

"Did you see the boy smile? Did you hear the boy speak?" Lily asks Lanlan. "Yes, I did. But he doesn't now."

Everyone goes back home. I stay in the classroom. I think hard. I want to know why Paul does not say anything to us. I try and try. I try again and again. Suddenly I find what can make Paul speak English.

步骤 2　分析故事

由于有明确的表演目的，所以学生阅读的心态不同于一般性阅读。教师一开始有必要花费一些时间进行故事分析的书面示范。

步骤3　文体转换

教师组织学生以小组活动的形式将故事文本改编为脚本。下面是改编的一个例子，改编由学生小组完成，经过教师点评，由小组再修改，最后由教师和学生共同定稿。

Act 1

Mr. White：Good morning，everyone.

Ss：Good morning.

Mr. White：I have a picture for you. It is a magic one. Look at the little boy in it.

（Mr. White says hello to the little boy in the picture.）

Mr. White：Hello，boy. Would you tell me your name，please?

Paul：Yes，sir. My name is Paul. I'm glad to see you，sir.

Ss：Wow，he can smile. He can speak English.

Lily：What a magic boy! What a magic picture!

（本场主要由Mr. White引出故事主角，并把他介绍给同学们。）

Act 2

Lily：Lanlan，come here.

Lanlan：What are you doing here?

Lily：I'm looking at the magic picture.

Lanlan：Paul is a magic boy. Let's talk to him.

Lily：Talk with us，Paul!

Lanlan：Talk，Paul!

（No answer.）

Li Gang：What are you doing here?

Lanlan：We want to make Paul talk in English.

Li Gang：Does he talk with you?

Lily：No，he doesn't.

Li Gang：Paul! Paul! Are you Paul?

（No answer.）

Liu Lei：Tell us，what's your name?

（No answer.）

Li Gang：Mr. White's picture is not a magic one. Paul can't speak English.

Lily：What a boy! He can't smile. He can't speak.

（Mr. White comes in.）

Mr. White：What's the matter?

Li Gang：Your boy can't smile. He can't speak.

Lily：He can't speak English. He can't answer our questions!

Mr. White：Is it true? Let me try. Paul，would you tell me your name，please?

Paul：I'm Paul. I'm your boy. I'm a magic boy.

Ss：Why?

Mr. White：He can speak English.

Ss：Oh，Mr. White，what's the matter?

Mr. White：I don't know. Think it over，children.

（本场展示的是故事的冲突：Paul 为什么呼应 Mr. White，而不呼应上场的几个同学?）

Act 3

(Only Lily stays in the classroom.)

Lily：Paul is a magic boy. Mr. White tells us he can speak English. We ask him questions. But he can't answer us. Why?

Paul，speak English! You must do it!

(No answer，Lily leaves. And Li Gang comes.)

Li Gang：(Looking at the picture) This picture is a magic one. Is it true?

Paul is a magic boy. Is it true? Paul，answer my questions. Are you Paul? Are you magic? Can you speak English? Open your mouth and tell me!

Tell me! Tell me! Tell me!

(No answer. Li Gang leaves. And Lanlan comes.)

Lanlan：(Speaking to herself) Paul is a magic boy. That is a magic picture. But the boy doesn't speak. Why? Why? Why? (Looking at the picture) Oh，Paul，please open your mouth and speak! Please do it! Please…

Paul：Hello，my friend. How are you?

Lanlan：Fine，thank you. (Shouting) Paul can speak English!

(Li Gang，Lily and Liu Lei come back.)

Ss：(cheering) Oh，Paul can speak English! Paul can speak English!

Li Gang：Sometimes Paul can. Sometimes Paul can't. Why?

Lily：Sometimes he speaks to somebody. Sometimes he doesn't speak to somebody else. Why?

Liu Lei：Paul answers some questions. But he doesn't answer other questions. Why?

（本场安排四个人出场，分别对Paul讲话，分别展示四人的困惑，并最终显示Paul回应了Lanlan，并就此再次提出问题，此问题在下一场得到解决。）

Act 4

(The four students come together and have a short meeting.)

Lily：How can we solve the problem?

Li Gang：I can tell you. Paul answers questions when he feels happy.

Lily：No，I don't think so. Why doesn't he answer anybody but Lanlan?

Li Gang：Because Lanlan is kind to him.

Lily：But I am kind to him，too.

Li Gang：But Lanlan has long hair. You have short hair.

Liu Lei：That's not the reason.

Lily：I think we can have a test!

Ss：Yes，let's have a test.

(The children gather together in front of the picture. The test begins.)

Lily：Boy，tell us your name!

(No answer)

Liu Lei：Boy，do as I tell you. What's your name? Say it now!

(No answer.)

Li Gang：I know your name is Paul. Can you speak English?

(No answer.)

Lanlan：Oh，Paul. Please open your mouth and speak!

Liu Lei：Please，please，Paul，open your mouth and speak!

Paul：Hello，boys and girls. I'm glad to meet you.

Ss：Oh，he speaks!

Paul：Hello，everyone.

Ss：(cheering) Oh，Paul opens his mouth and speaks!

Li Gang：Say it again!

(No answer.)

Ss：What's the matter?

Liu Lei：Open your mouth and speak!

(No answer.)

Open your mouth and speak，Paul，please!

Paul：Hello，everyone! I'm pleased to see you all.

Lily：Where do you come from?

（No answer.）

Where do you come from? Tell us，Paul，please!

Paul：I come from London.

Lanlan：Will you tell us a story?

（No answer.）

Will you tell us a story，please?

Paul：Yes，I will.

Li Gang：Oh，I've got it! When you say "please"，Paul will speak. When you don't，Paul won't.

（本场情节是：同学们通过检测找到了让 Paul 说话的"密码"，不管你想要 Paul 说什么，必须有 please 这个词，否则，他不会张口说话。）

Act 5

（The children sing and dance with Paul.）

Ss：Paul，Paul，please get on a bus，

And sit on a seat.

Paul，Paul，please sit on a seat，

And look at the street.

Paul，Paul，please bull the bell，

And make the bus stop.

Paul，Paul，please get off the bus，

And go to the toy shop.

（本场是故事的尾声，学生依照上面的歌曲与 Paul 一起跳舞唱歌，其中仍需不断地说 please。）

步骤 4　小组排练

挑选一位学生担任组长，主持排练活动。教师事先对组长进行必要的培训，突出排练的步骤，这样可以避免学生在排练时出现混乱。这些步骤包括：

（1）分担角色。

（2）分别练习台词。

（3）初次合演，并由学生导演。

（4）第二次合演，教师介入导演。

（5）正式表演。

注意事项：在排练中，教师应提醒学生串词只是排练的一部分，还要兼顾动作、表

情、位置和走动。

步骤 5　总结

(1) 发放本次活动涉及的语言知识项目表，供学生总结本次活动已使用的词汇和句型。这个语言项目表不仅仅包含故事本身的词汇和句型，也包括以往学过而在本活动中使用过的词汇和句型，同时还包括一些为了本活动的需要而使用的新词语。所以，一次故事表演所涉及的语言知识比一般的讲解课文的课堂活动所涉及的语言知识要丰富得多。

(2) 检查故事表演期间小组或个人撰写的脚本、讨论时的发言提纲以及故事分析提纲等等。

(3) 小组报告本次活动的情况，教师做口头或书面总结。

前面已经说过，教师在故事表演活动中担任总导演的角色，这一角色本身包含着教学指导的主要内容。下表可以清楚地表明导演功能和教学指导功能的双重意义：

故事表演	教师导演功能	教学指导功能	语言学习效果
学生改编故事	提供改编建议	写作指导	学生学习写作的具体技能
学生分析故事	参与表演及角色分工讨论	深层次理解与讨论	加强对原作的理解，评议改编的语言水平及问题
准备小组讨论及表演	提供排练步骤和角色分工的建议	师生进行真实的口头交流，使用新学的和已学的词汇与句型	培养口语技能，巩固语言知识
小组排练	现场对学生的语言和动作进行指导	在具体情境中练习角色的对话	培养口语技能，巩固语言知识，并随时学习新的语言知识
小组过场	进行动作和台词的指导	进行语音与语调的训练与指导，复习语言知识	培养口语技能，巩固语言知识，并随时学习新的语言知识
故事表演	充当舞台监督	在熟练掌握的基础上将语言知识和技能有机地融于特定的情境中	将已学过的语言知识运用于模拟实际生活的情境中，获得直接体验
总结	从导演的角度组织演员总结本次活动	总结和复习已学过的语言知识	系统总结本次活动的语言知识

第二节　游　戏

在应用环节中可以通过游戏将枯燥的语言知识变成让学生乐于接受的、生动有趣的知识，为学生创造丰富的语言交际情景，使学生在玩中学、在学中玩。互动语言教学认为小组活动有利于学生用目的语进行交际，而游戏就属于这种小组活动之一。

案例1

新知识：How are you…及其答语 I'm fine. Thank you. /Very well，thank you. 同时学会用 Let's…邀请朋友做事情。

在应用环节，教师设计了一个“两人接力”游戏：Let's paint! Great!（两个学生同时做动作，说出 Let's paint! Great! 一人贴星星，一人勾勒出星星的笑脸。）评出贴画星星最快的小组。

竞赛使学生学起来更有兴致，合作则培养了学生们的合作精神。

案例2

新知识：eye，ear，nose，mouth，leg，hair，face，knee，foot，arm，shoulder 等表示身体部位的词汇。

在应用环节，教师设计了这样一个游戏。

T：Now，let's play a game. Please do as I ask you to. For example，if I say，“Touch your nose.” please find and touch your nose with your finger and say，“I touch my nose.”

然后教师和全班同学一起做一次。

T：Touch your eyes.

S：I touch my eyes.

发命令的速度从慢到快，最后以最快的速度发出。

接着，教师请一位学生发出命令，教师和其他同学一起做，并同时大声重复命令。

最后，同桌之间轮流做 pair work。

案例3

新知识：英语元音中的长元音和短元音。

在应用环节，教师设计了这样一个游戏。

教师在黑板上写出一组含有长元音和短元音的单词（此组词中所有单词的开始音和结束音都是相同的辅音，不同的是各自元音的长短，0，3，8 是长元音，其余的是短元音）。如下：

PORT	PIT	PAT	PERT	PET
0	1	2	3	4
POT	PUTT	PUT	PART	PEAT
5	6	7	8	9

教师示范每一个单词的发音，学生重复。接着，教师示范每个词中的元音发音，学生重复。多次示范和跟读，直到学生基本熟悉单词的发音和长短音的区别。

教师读上面的词汇，学生听并写出相对应的数字编码。然后教师公布正确答案，学生互相纠正、比较对错。教师纠正学生混淆的元音。接着教师一次把 2～3 个表中单词一起读，学生听并写出相对应的数字编码。

之后，教师一次把 6 个表中的单词一起读，学生听并写出相对应的数字编码。接着学生配对练习多个词，并写出相应的数字。

游戏结束后，可每组选一位学生，大声读出与自己在游戏中记下的数字相对应的单词，请其他同学根据读音写出自己的一串数字，然后公布答案，学生互相纠正。在这个过程中，学生会有很多争论和纠正，比如“You said…”“No，I didn't!”“Say it again.”等等。教师可以边观察边示范正确读音。

案例 4

新知识：最新沪教版五年级下学期的教材中安排了一个文化单元：Holidays。教师在教授了各种西方节日名称后，可以让学生在课堂上或课后开展一些与节日活动相关的游戏。比如，制作复活节彩蛋，绘制圣诞卡，做南瓜灯，等等。教师要注意的是，文化课的教学不应当只介绍国外文化，在传授新知识的同时，也应该帮助学生加深对本国或本地区的独特文化的理解。

第三节　调　查

用英语做调查能培养学生用英语解决问题的能力。虽然小学阶段所学内容不多，但可以设计简单的、易操作的调查。例如，在学习了有关食物的单词，知道有西餐和中餐后，可以设计一个调查表，让学生调查同学当中喜欢吃中餐和西餐的比例。全班同学分成 4 组，每组制作一个表格，上面写有同学的名字，还写有食品的名称：Hot dog，Fries，Hamburgers，Dumplings，Noodles，让学生拿着调查表在组内用“Do you like…?”展开调查。喜欢的打“√”，不喜欢的打“×”，然后把调查结果统计出来。学生在汇报时还可提出少吃快餐食品、注意营养合理搭配等建议。

案例 1

《新交际英语》第五册第三单元 Where Are You From 一课的主要内容是询问某人是何地人或哪国人的日常交际用语。在应用环节，教师设计了一个调查：

T：Do you have good friends? Do you want to make new friends?

Ss：Yes.

T：Now you can interview your classmates or teachers around you. But remember this. You are not yourself. You are another person. Look at this paper. You are Tom. You're 22 years old. You are a bus driver. You like Britain. You can ask your classmates or teachers to make friends with you. These sentences can help you：

May I know your name? /Excuse me，what's your name? /what's your name please?

Where are you from? /where do you come from? /Are you from…? How old are you? What's your job? What country do you like? Do you like China?

（教师给学生准备了12个不同身份的资料，让学生把自己的信息告诉新朋友，并通过对话获取新朋友的信息。）

T：Ok. I think you have some new friends now. How many new friends do you have? Would you come here，Jack?

S1：Three.

T：Can you say something about your new friends?

S1：Let me have a try. Tommy is from Australia. He's 35. He's a driver. He likes China. Sue is 51. She's a shop keeper. She's from Canada. She loves China. Miss Yao is a teacher. She is Chinese. She wants to go to Japan.

T：Good job. Now please choose one of your new friend and introduce him or her to your classmates in your group.

（教师先让一个学生出来介绍他的新朋友的情况，再让同学们在小组里就各自新朋友的情况进行交流。）

（The pupils shared their information with others.）

第四节　动画电影

动画电影的使用，能给学生提供角色模仿的模型。通过教授语言的合适性和文化性，教师可以增加学生的文化意识，加强学生的视觉和听觉理解能力。

“所有的儿童天生具有一种吸收文化的能力。”“如果儿童生活在一个有文化的环境里，环境就会丰富他的词汇。”儿童学习英语，环境是非常重要的。动画电影中的直观画面给学生理解和学习文化提供了语境信息，其色彩和情节能激发小学生了解和学习文化的兴趣。英语动画电影能够展现学习者感兴趣的英语国家的文化习俗和价值观念，促进文化学习和语言学习的共同发展，因为电影可以为图式背景知识的发展提供重要的支持。在应用环节使用动画电影不仅能让小学生看到和听到真实语境中的真实语言，而且能让小学生观察到真实的语言交往模式。

放映动画电影的常用方法有：

放映无字幕的动画电影，让学生通过画面和人物的动作猜测动画电影的大意。

放映带有目标语关键词字幕的动画电影片段，使学生熟练应用所学词汇。

放映动画电影片段，训练语音语调。

放映带有中英文字幕的动画电影，阅读动画片的台词，了解动画片的整体内容。

放映带有英语字幕的动画电影，根据动画的剧情进行猜测。

放映带有英语字幕的动画电影，模仿练习。

放映带有英语字幕的动画电影，做角色扮演。

放映带有英语字幕的动画电影，对比发音。

放映带有英语字幕的动画电影，配音练习。

案例

新知识：Animal School

There are no classes in Animal School，but there are a big forest and a small river.

Mr. Owl：What's the matter?

Little Rabbit：I'm sad. I can't swim. And I can't climb trees. I'm a bad student.

Mr. Owl：I don't think so. Please don't be sad.

Animals：Come on，everyone! Let's run together!

Mr. Owl：Have a try，Little Rabbit! You can run very well.

Animals：Wow! Look at Little Rabbit! He is so fast!

Little Rabbit：I'm the first! I'm so happy!

在应用环节，教师提供了《功夫熊猫》和《里约大冒险》两个动画电影片段，向学生展示了 animal school 中另外两个小动物——熊猫 Po 和蓝金刚鹦鹉 Blu 的问题和烦恼，让学生在巩固核心语言、体验语言运用的过程中，丰富语言的表述，强化语言的实践和解决问题的体验。

以下是根据动画电影片段教师再构的对话文本：

《功夫熊猫》

Master shifu：What's wrong?

Po：I'm too fat. I eat vegetables everyday. But I'm still fat.

Tiger：Keep smiling.

Master shifu：Believe in yourself. Why not try it again?

Po：OK. I'll have a try. Let's learn Kungfu.

《里约大冒险》

Rafael：Are you Ok?

Blu：I can't fly，I'm afraid. It's too high.

Jewel：Come on. Don't give up.

Parrot：Don't worry! Look at me. My wings are short but I can do it. I think you'd better have a try.

Blu：OK. Let's go.

第七章

结课环节的设计

本章导读

常言道，“善始善终”才算一堂优质课。良好的开头虽然是成功的一半，但完善精要的结尾，犹如“画龙点睛”，会使课堂教学再起波澜，从而给教学活动画上一个完美的句号。因此，精心设计结课这一教学环节，对于良好教学效果的巩固有着举足轻重的作用。一般来说，结课环节包括复习巩固、布置作业等内容。

第一节　复习巩固

案例 1

沪教版《英语》(牛津版) 5B Module 2 Unit 1 Animals in the Zoo

教学目标：

1. 在具体的情境中能运用新句型“How much … do the … eat?”和“How many kilos…?”。

2. 了解动物的一些习性。

3. 运用所学句型描述动物。

教学结束活动：

Ask some questions to get some information about an animal from your desk mates.

A	B
I know: Look at the elephants. They come from Yunnan province. They like to eat hay. They eat about 100 kilos of hay every day. They can play with their noses. I think it's very interesting.	**I know:** Look at the tigers. They come from the northeast of China. They like to eat meat. They eat about 10 kilos of meat every day. They are fierce. But they are sad because they are facing to the danger of extinction (灭绝).
Ask your partner to get information: Tigers Look at the tigers. They come from ________. They like to eat ________. They eat about ________ every day. They are ________. But they are sad because they are facing to the danger of extinction (灭绝).	**Ask your partner to get information:** Elephants Look at the elephants. They come from ________ province. They like to eat ________. They eat about ________ every day. They can ________. I think it's very interesting.

案例的教学目标要求学生能运用刚学的新句型和丰富的语言描述动物。因此，从教学目标出发，教师在结课环节设计安排了对子活动，以 AB 表的方式，利用信息差，让学生通过提问等相互交流的形式，获取他们自己所需要的信息，在提升学生阅读能力的同时，又在具体的语境中进一步巩固操练了新学的句型。

英语课堂教学活动关注从机械的练习到有意义的操练，然后到交际的教学过程。从整节课活动安排考虑，结束环节中的活动是这节课中梯度最高的。

第二节　布置作业

小学英语作业的布置是一门艺术，精心设计的作业不仅能使学生所学的知识在系统梳理的基础上得以升华，而且还能使学生在乐中学、在学中乐，不断激起学生智慧的火花。

一、小学英语作业布置常见的问题

小学英语作业布置常见的问题有：

（1）作业单调、枯燥。以读、背、抄、写等机械性题型为主，偏重课本，内容重复。机械操练死记硬背加重了学生的负担，与素质教育背道而驰，不符合新课标的要求。

（2）随意布置作业。有的教师布置作业缺乏目标意识，随意布置作业，重数量忽视质量，结果劳而无功。

（3）作业形式单一。以选择填空的形式居多，缺乏层次性，不利于学生听、说、读、写能力的综合发展。

二、小学英语作业布置的尝试

1. 词汇作业

通过某些灵活或艺术的形式布置词汇作业能极大地激发学生的学习兴趣。具体的形式有：

（1）画图表达。如在教了介词 on，in，under 后，可以让学生课后画三幅画，分别表示这三个介词，并且就每幅画写一个句子。如：

A

B

C

A. There are many books in the box.

B. A boy is standing on the chair and cleaning the window.

C. There is a cat under the table.

（2）动作演示。学生借助肢体语言演示单词。如在学了动词 swim，jump，run，hop 后，可以让学生课后边做动作边说单词，第二天课堂上让学生来演示，也可采取让学生做动作，其他同学来猜一猜的方式。

（3）英语小贴士。针对与生活密切相关的英语单词，如 pencil-box，ruler，wallet，scarfs，doll，mirror 等，让学生适时制作小贴士贴在相关的物件上。这类作业可促使学生多接触英语单词，还可以锻炼书写和提高审美能力。

（4）单词故事。让学生编一个故事，里面要用到新学的单词。如在学了 father，mother，teacher，driver，student，family 后，让学生编一个故事。此作业既可加深学生对所学单词的理解，又可提高语言表达能力。

2. 听读作业

“听读作业”是指为提高学生的听、读语言技能而布置的作业，设计时要凸显其科学性、艺术性和有效性，减少盲目性。

（1）听课文。可分 A、B、C 三个层次让学生自主选择。A 层次要求在听课文的基础上进行换词对话表演，B 层次要求听熟会背，C 层次要求跟着录音原原本本地听读。这样一来，不同层次的学生可以根据自己的具体情况选择相应的作业并充分展示自我，这对学生听读积极性的保护起到了关键性的作用。

现行小学英语教科书的课文都配有录音磁带，它语言地道、纯正、规范，是最好的听力材料。布置听读作业有以下要求：一周五天，每天 10 分钟左右，反复听本周所学的那一单元的对话内容。周一、周二以听为主，周三、周四边听边跟读，随着教学内容的推进，到周五基本上会背，这样既延长了学生接触英语的时间，又能让学生在熟悉课文内容的基础上反复跟读，加深记忆，增强语感，这是提高听力水平的有效方法之一。

（2）读课文。在英语教学中，为了让学生掌握标准的语音语调，要经常让学生听录音，在此基础上，再让学生有感情地朗读课文并做好录音，然后将录制下来的录音在课堂上播放。在录制前，学生们总会集中精神，认真朗读课文，反复操练，直到自己满意为止。这种作业在很大程度上调动了学生的积极性，激发了他们的学习兴趣，也为学生的口语表达能力打下了坚实的基础。更重要的是，这种形式的作业既避免了学生抄写作业的现象，使学生在潜移默化中形成较强的语感，又提高了作业质量。

3. 口语作业

（1）表演对话。英语教学的任务不仅要求学生能开口讲英语，而且还要为学生提供语言实践的机会。由于课外让学生开口老师很难监控，课堂便成了教会学生开口的主要场所。在课堂上教授某一对话内容后，可以给学生布置小组合作表演的作业。如就人教版《英语》（PEP 版）四年级（上）Unit 5B Let's Talk 的内容，教师可让学生 4 人一组担当不同的角色，在大家熟悉对话内容的基础上再按“情节”合演。基础较好的学生还可做扩展对话表演，表演时教师可允许学生准备服装及道具，还可让他们模仿动画片中人物的动作进行表演。由于这类作业是学生们感兴趣的，同学们会踊跃参加。这不仅保证了每个学生都有开口的机会，而且极大地激发了学生的学习兴趣。

（2）自由对话。要求学生每周分组做一次自由对话练习。内容包括星期、日期、天气、出勤、各自的家庭情况、兴趣爱好和周围发生的有趣的事情。比如，教完如何打电话这一课后，教师可以给学生设置一个模拟场景，准备两部电话，让学生学习用英语打个电话，复习当天学过的单词和句型，这种形式的作业，气氛活跃，学生参与度高，效果自然不错。

4. 自助餐作业

新课程倡导充分发挥学生主体的积极性、主动性和创造性。教师布置作业时可以根据学生的差异将作业设计成难易有别的 A、B、C、D 等组别，让学生根据自己的实际情况选择做。形式多样的“自助餐”式作业能使学生在原有的基础上各有收获，享受到成功的喜悦。如在学习了“My Friend”后，教师可以设计 5 项作业：（1）爱写作的你，不妨用英语写一篇小文章介绍你的好朋友。（2）爱诵读的你，不妨有感情地朗读 My friend，然后录音。（3）爱画画的你，不妨根据课文里的描述，画一画你的好朋友。（4）爱讲故事的你，不妨把课文改编成英语小故事，讲给父母听。（5）爱观察的你，不妨好好观察你的同学，找出他们的特点，设计成英语小谜语让同学们猜猜。

这一组作业设计包含了“读、画、写、编、讲”五种形式，既给爱画、爱读的学生提供了展示自己本领的空间，又为爱探索、爱讲故事的学生提供了进一步锻炼自己的机会。一项作业能使学生各展所长，使学生的创新思维得到发挥。

5. 拓展作业

拓展教学资源能发展学生的语言思维能力。比如课文里只有两个句子：What's your favorite animal? I like sheep/ducks…，但通过教学资源的有效拓展和学生的自我意义建构，学生介绍自己喜爱的动物就会如数家珍。再辅以竞赛的形式以及“和小动物交朋友”的角色扮演活动，学生表达欲望会更强烈，新的句子不断脱口而出，请看下面两个学生的对话。

S1：What's your favorite animal?

S2：Look，I like polar bear.

S1：Why?

S2：Because it's cute. It looks white and fat. But its eyes and nose are black. It eats fish and it can swim.

最后，作业是将从网上收集的动物资料整理成配图文章。

案例 1

沪教版《英语》(牛津版) 3B Module 2 Unit 2 Lovely Animals

Homework：

（第一次教学）

1. Say something about animals with your parents.
2. Try to know more about other animals.

（第二次教学）

Step 1

Say something about animals with your parents.

Try to know more about other animals.

Step2

Watch the video，think about the following questions：

What can kangaroos do?

What do they like to eat?

Where do they live?

在日常课堂教学中，类似于第一次教学中的作业布置对教师来说也许司空见惯，教师的关注点在于“布置”，其中的“Try to know more about other animals”对于大多数学生

而言，没有明确的要求，缺乏操作性，也难以实施。

在第二次教学中，教师进行了行为改进，重心下移。教师布置作业后，随即举例，以袋鼠做示范，让学生欣赏关于袋鼠的短片视频。多元化的体验让学生了解了袋鼠的生活习性，从而引发了学生更浓厚的了解其他动物的兴趣，拓展延伸从课内到课外，唤起学生的思维意识。同时在欣赏的过程中让学生带着问题观看，关键性的问题引导学生在课外观看时更有目的和方向。

案例 2

沪教版《英语》（牛津版）5A Module 3　Unit 2　Let's Go Shopping

教学目标：

1. 能在具体的情境中运用 be interested in something 表述购物兴趣。
2. 能在语境、语段中理解 shopping season，on sale，shopping mall。
3. 了解本地的一些购物特色，制作购物小贴士，激发学生热爱家乡、热爱生活的情感。

Homework：

1. Enjoy a video about shopping places in×××.
2. Match the places and the special shopping stuff.
3. Give some tips to the new teachers in our school.

Shopping tips

Hello，________，let me help you.
×××is a ________ place for shopping.
If you're interested in ____________，
you can go to ______________.
There is/are ______________ in it.
Come on，enjoy your life in ×××!

关于“购物”的话题，传统的情感教育方式往往会想到教育学生不能乱花钱，如果游离于学生的情感体验，对学生进行教育难免会弄巧成拙。

本节课作业的设计从一般的逻辑思维中找出了情感教育的张力点，把情感教育目标定位于：了解本地的一些购物特色，通过制作购物小贴士，激发学生热爱家乡、热爱生活的情感。教师让学生通过欣赏有关本地购物特色的视频，获取信息，了解地方购物生活，结合实际，感悟、体验购物乐趣，并为自己身边的新教师制作购物小贴士。在制作购物小贴士的过程中，学生不仅对新知识进行综合运用，又自然而然地被情感教育渗透。

三、改进作业的评价方式

在日常工作中，许多老师往往把作业批改当成是例行公事，喜欢用一把尺子量所有的同学，作业评价只起了检查的功能，忽视了评价的激励作用。对学生的作业，简单地打上“√”“×”或“A”“B”“C”了事。长此以往，作业中的错误得不到纠正，出现的精彩得不到赏识，结果学生对待作业的态度越来越马虎。如果有一天，老师在他们的作业本或默写本上不再是打“A”“B”“C”或分数，而是画上他们意想不到的大拇指、笑脸、哭脸、星星等等，又或是老师亲笔写上的“Very good! Well done! Good job! Excellent! Great! Try again!”等等，学生定会无比高兴，互相炫耀，下次的作业定会加倍认真，而且会急切盼望着下次的作业老师会有什么不一样的评价。

四、组织有效的作业展评活动

为了提高学生做作业的积极性，每月举办一次优秀作业展评活动，把作业质量最高或作业进步大的同学的作业展示在班级的墙报上。这样一来，每个学生都希望自己的作业能被展览，从而提高了做作业的积极性，激发了做作业的热情。除了对书面作业进行展评以外，教师也要充分地挖掘出背书、默写单词、预习等的优秀者，如背书快的授予“背书小能手”称号，默写快而准的授予“单词王”称号，善于预习的授予“预习标兵”称号，造句好的授予“造句冠军”……小学生好胜心强，爱表现自己，暂时“落后”的同学会奋起直追，努力提高自己作业的质量。

第八章

案例解析

本章导读

本章将就语音教学、词汇教学、句型教学、对话教学和语篇教学提供案例，并对案例从准备环节、呈现环节、操练环节、应用环节和结课环节进行全方位的解析。

第一节　语音教学

案例 1

《英语》(PEP 版) 3B Unit 3 How Many

Step 1　Warming up

T：Good morning，boys and girls.

Ss：Good morning，Miss Gong.

T：How are you?

Ss：Fine，thank you.

T：Now let's sing a song "One Two Three Four Five".

Step 2　Presentation

T：Look. I have three books. How many books do you have?

S1：I have two books.

T：Good. Now eyes on the screen. How many spoons can you see?

S2：I can see thirteen spoons.

T：You are so clever. Follow me. Thirteen，thirteen. Three，thirteen.

教师板书：three——thirteen

T：Follow me. ee/iː/

T：You have a try.

S3：Four，Fourteen. Five，fifteen.

教师板书：four——fourteen

five——fifteen

T：Six.

Ss：sixteen.

T：seven.

Ss：seventeen.

T：eight.

Ss：eighteen.

T：nine.

Ss：nineteen.

T：Great.

Step 3　Practice

T：Pair work.

S4：Three.

S5：Thirteen.

S6：Four.

S7：Fourteen.

……

T：Please write down what I said. Three apples；thirteen crayons；four bananas；fourteen pencils；five pears；fifteen dogs；six oranges；sixteen dolls；seven pineapples；seventeen lamps；eight eggs；eighteen basketballs；nine melons；nineteen footballs.

（请7个小朋友写在黑板上）

Guessing game：

（将全班分成若干小组，每组抽一个人到前面去，背对着班级。教师拿一个袋子，向同学们借一些书本、铅笔、橡皮、硬币等放入袋中，然后让已经上前的各组学生轮流猜袋子里东西的数目，猜对的给该组记10分。）

Step 4　Production

A survey：

How many…do you have?

（把学生分成五人或六人一组，给每人一张调查表格，让他们用“How many…do you have?”来询问同伴，并根据同伴的回答填写表格。）

	story books	crayons	pencils	balls
Tom				
Mary				
Alice				
Ellen				
Summer				

Step 5　Summing up

Homework：

（1）Draw 3 and 13 animals you like. Describe them to your parents.

（2）Write a rhyme with 3，13，4，14，5，15，6，16，7，17，8，18，9，19.

案例1解析

小学英语语音教学的任务不是让小学生学些语音理论，而是教会小学生运用英语语音的基本知识，发展听、说、读、写的基本能力，培养对英语的语言感觉。这堂课很好地贯彻了这一点。

在准备环节，教师和同学们亲切问好，营造了温馨的氛围，为上课做好准备。

在呈现环节，教师通过展示屏呈现数字13，然后通过单音示范→结合单词示范→对比其他音示范→书写到黑板上示范→讲解怎样发音→学生集体模仿→学生单个模仿→教师纠正，使要点和难点具体、简单、明了。此外，呈现环节还体现了教师重视字母组合读音规则的学习，这有利于学生形成见词直接呼读、迅速正确拼单词的能力。

在操练环节，教师通过 pair work 进一步巩固了学生对单词拼读规则的认识，游戏活动既活跃了气氛，又使同学们在真实的语境中熟练表达英语数字。多种多样的操练形式，调动了学生的学习积极性。同时，在各种趣味操练中，学生初步掌握了英语字母的拼读规则。

在应用环节，教师巧妙地设计了一张调查表，为学生的语言交流提供了语言材料，使同学们进一步熟悉了句型“How many…do you have?”“How many…does he/she have?”，并对数字的正确发音有了更深的认知。

在结课环节，这堂课的作业布置设计新颖，具有实践性，有利于提高学生的口语交际能力。

案例 2

《英语》(PEP 版) 4B Unit 2 Part C

Step 1 Warming up

T：Good morning，boys and girls.

Ss：Good morning，teacher.

T：Let's sing “ABC” song together.

Step 2 Presentation

T：How many letters are there in English? How many vowel letters are there in English? What are they?

S1：There are 26 letters in English. There are 5 vowel letters in English. They are a，e，i，o，u.

T：Good. Today we will learn two vowel letters：a and e.

T：Look at the pictures. What does “a” sound like in these words?

T：A sounds like/ei/in cake. You have a try.

S2：A sounds like/ei/in grape.

S3：A sounds like/ei/in face.

S4：A sounds like/ei/in snake.

T：What does a sound like in these words：

apple bag cat hat

S5：A sounds like/æ/in apple，bag，cat and hat.

T：Well-done. Follow me. /æ/，/æ/，apple，↗，apple. ↙

Now look at the pictures. What does e sound like in these words?

T：E sounds like/e/in bed. You have a try.

S6：E sounds like/e/in pen.

S7：E sounds like/e/in desk.

S8：E sounds like/e/in egg.

T：What does e sound like in these words：

we　　me　　she　　he

S9：E sounds like/iː/in we，me，she，he.

T：Excellent. Follow me. /iː/，/iː/，me，↗ me. ↙

Step 3　Practice

（1）看动作猜音标。

（2）看口型猜音标。

（3）听音标举卡片：教师准备若干音标卡片，然后教师以 show me your/ei/，show me your/æ/，show me your/iː/，show me your/e/提问。

（4）听单词举音标卡片：教师准备单词卡片若干。教师举单词卡片 cake（可替换），让学生找字母 a 在单词 cake 中的发音并举起相应的音标卡片。

Step 4　Production

（1）Game "Find your home".

/ei/　　/æ/　　/iː/　　/e/

（教师把全班分成四个小组，准备单词卡片若干，要求学生帮四个音标找到它们的家人并贴在该房子下，最先完成且没有错误的为优胜。）

（2）Say a rhyme.

/ei//ei//ei/Say "Ok".

/æ//æ//æ/Look at the blackboard.

/iː//iː//iː/Drink some tea.

/e//e//e/Let it rest.

Step 5　Summing up

T：What did you learn in this class?

We learned a's and e's pronunciation.

A/ei/cake，grape，face，snake.

A/æ/apple，bag，cat，hat.

E/e/bed，pen，desk，egg.

E/iː/we，me，she，he.

Let's say it together.

Homework：

（1）找一找，还有哪些含有字母 a 的单词发/ei/和/æ/的音。

（2）找一找，还有哪些含有字母 e 的单词发/e/和/iː/的音。

案例 2 解析

这堂课的重点是让学生能够听懂、会说、会读音标/ei/，/æ/，/iː/，/e/和单词 cake，snake，grape，face，apple，bag，cat，hat，we，me，she，he，bed，pen，desk，egg。

在准备环节，师生共唱“ABC”，缓解了学生课前的紧张情绪，营造了和谐的英语学习氛围，同时为新课教学做了铺垫。

在呈现环节，教师通过直观教学法让学生感知、体验，自己总结出元音字母 a 在单词中的发音规律，并且使新旧知识得到整合。在教授音标的时候，教师示范口型，要求学生仔细听音，观察口型，认真模仿，这样一来，学生就可以感知英语的语音、语调，这是一个由观察到复制再到自由地创造性运用英语的过程。

在操练环节，教师通过看、猜、听、举的活动，不断训练学生对语音的敏感度，同时，生动活泼的形式增强了学生的形象记忆，促进了语音教学过程的优化，让学生在愉快中收获成功的自信。

在应用环节，教师通过“找家人”的游戏让学生亲自参与体验，游戏和合作的方式能激发学生的学习兴趣，同时还锻炼了学生的分析能力和记忆能力。此外顺口溜使知识变得简单、生动、印象深刻，而且这样的训练能够真正将语音教学落到实处。

在结课环节，教师再次总结知识要点，所布置的作业起到了启发学生思考的作用。

第二节 词汇教学

案例 1

广东版《英语》4A Friends with English

Step 1 Warming up

T：Good morning，boys and girls. Let's sing a song together. "What do you like?"

Step 2 Presentation

T：Look! This is a basket and there are some fruits，stationaries and balls in it. Tom，do you like the yellow ball?

Tom：No，I like the green one.

T：Linda，what do you like?

Linda：I like to eat apples.

T：Look! Gogo is busy helping students in the library. Now we will select some excellent students to help him. Do you want to have a try?

Ss：Yes!

T：All right. If you want to succeed，you must finish two tasks. A. Who's good at learning? B. Who's good at acting?

T：First，let's learn new words and sentences. Please show me your books.

Ss：Book!

T：What book，what book? An English book.

T：Look at the photo，please. Who's she?

S1：She's Miss Fang.

T：I'm your English teacher. Is she your English teacher?

S1：No，she isn't.

S：Yes. She's your math teacher.

T：Look! What's that?

S2：It's a piano.

T：Who can play piano?

S3：I can.

T：Good. Let's listen to the music.

（学生演奏完简短一曲后）

T：The music is very nice. Do you think so?

Ss：Yes!

（显示屏呈现美术课片段）

T：Is it a music lesson?

Ss：No.

T：It's the art lesson. In the art lesson，we can draw and paint. What can we do in the P. E. lesson.

S4：We can run，jump，play basketball，play ping-pong…

T：（戴上魔术帽）Hello，boys and girls. I'm the magician. I have magic power. Look at the paper. There's no word on it，right?

Ss：Yes.

（教师施"魔法"，在事先用粥水写过单词的纸上涂上碘，"science"马上显现出来。）

T：Now there's a word on it! Listen to the tape and read the word together.

Step 3　Practice

T：Let's have a chant.

English，English，A B C；

Math，math，1 2 3；

Music，music，Do Re Mi；

Art，art，paint，paint，paint；

P. E.，P. E.，I like you；

Science，science，great，great，great!

Step 4　Production

（显示屏呈现一学生向Gogo借书的情景。）

Gogo：Hello!

Ann：Hi!

Gogo：What do you like?

Ann：I like English.

Gogo：Do you like this English book?

Ann：Yes，I do.

Gogo：OK. Here you are.

Ann：Thank you.

Gogo：You're welcome. Bye.

Ann：Bye-bye.

Group work.（每一组就是一个图书室，学生纷纷拿出各种图书，有的扮演图书管理员，有的扮演借书者，各自开展对话。通过自评、互评，学生选出自己小组中最好的一位。被选出的6位同学自行组合，在课室一角的“图书室”进行对话表演，最后师生共同评价，选出最好的3位当图书管理员。）

Step 5　Summing up

Read the words and the sentences again.

Homework:

(1) Listen to the tape and read the words and the sentences.

(2) Copy the new words.

(3) Ask your friends or your relatives, what subjects do they like? And finish the form.

案例1解析

这堂课的重点词汇是English，math，music，art，P. E. 和science。

在准备环节，教师和学生一起唱歌曲“What do you like”，很快将学生的注意力吸引到课堂，并创设了一种轻松、和谐的氛围。

在呈现环节，教师先拿出装有水果、文具和各种球的篮子，向学生一一呈现，复习相关单词，然后问个别学生“Do you like …?”“What do you like?”这样既拉近了师生间的距离，又巩固了旧知识，为新授知识做好了铺垫。接着教师展示课件，屏幕上出现Gogo在图书室为同学借书，忙得不可开交的场景，以此引出总任务：选几名优秀的同学当图书管理员，帮Gogo完成借书的任务。想要当选，必须过两关：(1) Who's good at learning? (2) Who's good at acting? 明确要求后，教师开始教单词：通过请同学们拿出英语课本自然而然地引出第一门学科English，之后通过出示一张照片引出第二门学科Math，最妙的是请一位同学演奏钢琴，这使同学们一下子记住了第三门学科——Music，同时让学生展示了艺术才华，在英语课上“秀”了一把。Art通过屏幕展示也是一个不错的方法。P. E. 的呈现略显单调。最棒的是最后一门学科——Science的呈现，教师俨然成了一位魔术师，魔术表演很好地诠释了科学这门学科的价值。总体来说，这堂课的词汇教学体现了前后连贯、衔接自然、形式多样、新颖别致的特色。鉴于这6个单词比较抽象，教师还自编了chant，并配以手势和动作，在教师的带动下，学生按节拍、按韵律说得朗朗上口，以生动、形象的形式强化了单词的记忆。

在操练环节，教师主要通过Pair work的形式让学生巩固所学的词汇。

在应用环节，教师通过Group work让每个小组成立一个“图书室”。在开放、包容的合作氛围中，学生相互激励，相互促进，各展所长，人人参与，个个体验。教师通过任务，以“动”促说、以“动”促用，使学生真正学以致用。

这堂课的结课环节比较简单，作业布置重视基础性训练，但趣味性和启发性还不够。

案例2

牛津小学英语（上海版）4A Module 2 Unit 2 Visiting a Fire Station

Step 1　Warming up

T：Hello，boys and girls.

Ss：Hello，Jessica.

T：In the previous lessons，we knew some jobs. Do you know any jobs?

S1：I know accountant.

S2：I know journalist.

S3：I know engineer.

T：Good. But do you know who he is?

S4：He is Yao Ming.

T：Yes. Do you like Yao Ming? What does he do?

S5：I like Yao Ming. He is a famous basketball player.

T：Yes. But he also can do many different jobs. Do you want to know? Let's watch the movie.

S6：He is a taxi-driver and a farmer.

S7：He can play the drum very well.

S8：He is a journalist.

T：Good. He is also a wild animal trainer. What do you want to be in the future? Why?

S9：I want to be an English teacher because I like English.

S10：I want to be a nurse because I can take care of the patients.

T：I hope your dream will come true. Do you know in the USA，what do many children want to be? Can you guess?

S11：Maybe they want to be directors.

Step 2　Presentation

T：No，you can find the answer in the passage. Now，listen carefully.

S12：They want to be firefighters.

T：Good! And how are the firefighters?

S13：They're brave and strong.

T：Yes. What can they do about the fire?

S14：They can save people from the fire.

T：Yes. Do you know how many firefighters died on September 11th，2001?

S15：343 firefighters died on September 11th，2001.

T：Do you like firefighters?

Ss：Yes.

T：I know one firefighter. Look! This is Mr Li. He is a firefighter. Today，let's follow Mr Li to visit a fire station.

T：Read after me. Visiting a fire station.

T：What is a fire station? What can you see?

（显示屏呈现消防车）

S16：I can see a red car.

T：Yes. You can see the number 119. There is an important thing at the fire station. What is it? Listen.

S17：Fire engine.

T：Thank you. Read after me. Fire engine，fire engine.

T：Fire engine is very important to firefighters. What does fire engine have? Listen carefully.

S18：A ladder and an ax.

T：Excellent. Follow me. Ladder，ladder. Ax，ax.

S19：It has a hose.

T：Good. Hose，hose.

T：Firefighters can use an ax to open the door. They can use a ladder to help people come out from a tall building. They use a hose to put out fires.

Step 3　Practice

T：Now，I put all the things into a rhyme.

Engine，engine，fire engine.

There is a ladder，an ax and a hose.

They use a ladder，an ax and a hose.

They use a ladder to help people.

They use an ax to open the door.

They use a hose to put out fires.

Fire，fire，they put out fires.

T：Firefighters put out fires. They're so cool. But the fire is dangerous. What can keep the firefighters safe? Let's watch. What does a firefighter have?

S20：He has a coat，a pair of boots，a mask and a helmet.

T：Look at the helmet. How does it feel? Why do firefighters need it?

Ss：They wear it to keep their heads safe.

（显示屏呈现消防头盔、防护服、防护靴、防毒面具）

Ss：They wear the coat to keep their bodies safe.

They wear the boots to keep their feet safe.

They wear the mask to keep their faces safe.

Step 4　Production

T：Now，choose one equipment you like and tell me what is this? How does it feel? Why do you wear it?

(教师拿出事先准备好的装备)

S21：Look. This is my coat. It's red. I wear it to keep my body safe.

S22：Look. This is my mask. It's hard. I wear it to keep my face safe.

S23：Look. This is my boots. They're smooth and soft. I wear them to keep my feet safe.

T：Very good. Fire is so dangerous. How can we avoid starting a fire? I have some tips for you. Which tip is for picture one?

S24：Don't play with the fire.

S25：Get low and go out of the building. It's for picture two. And picture three：make an escape plan.

T：Yes. You can make an escape plan like this，you can draw the routes you want to go. Maybe through the door or the window. But if unfortunately you meet a fire，what can you do? Now take out your paper. I have a little passage for you. Read it and match the sign with the tips.

Use the stairs.

Get low and go outside.

Don't go back.

Step 5　Summing up

T：OK. Just now we visited a fire station. What have you learnt? Question time. What can you see at a fire station?

Ss：We can see a fire engine.

T：What does the fire engine have?

Ss：It has a ladder，an ax and a hose.

T：What does a firefighter have?

Ss：He has a coat，a mask，a pair of boots and a helmet.

T：When you see the fire，what can you do? Who can act?

（教师拿出毛毯）

A boy acts：Close the door and put a blanket or a quilt at the foot of the door. Open the window and shout "help". Let people know that you're inside.

Homework：

（1）Read the story and copy new words.

（2）Get more information about fire safety from our school website.

案例2解析

这堂课的重点词汇是 fire engine，ladder，ax，hose，mask，helmet。

在准备环节，教师先通过姚明担当不同职业角色的视频引发同学们思考自己对未来职业的向往。

在呈现环节，教师通过另一段视频向学生展示了"9·11"事件后美国儿童心目中的英雄和对未来职业的向往——消防员。这一呈现方式令人印象深刻，它极大地勾起了学生想了解消防员这一职业的愿望，培养了学生的高尚情操。接着，教师通过视频带领大家参观消防站，逐一介绍了词汇 fire engine，ladder，ax，hose。在教 hose 时，教师还引导学生根据 nose 的发音自己试着念一念。

在操练环节，教师通过编写韵律感极强的 chant 巩固了新学的词汇，但操练的形式略显单一。

在应用环节，教师通过图片展示消防员装备的实物——消防头盔、防护服、防护靴和防毒面具使学生又学会了两个新词：mask，helmet。用这种活用实物的方法教词汇会使学生觉得很亲近，从而使他们更能融入课堂中去。接着教师让学生通过演一演的方式进一步巩固新学的词汇。这堂课的应用环节是重头戏，教师通过一定的多媒体手段创设了真实语境，激发学生主动地去记忆词汇，使词汇教学更有效，使学生更有劲，也使教学过程更完整。

在结课环节，教师先通过 Question time 复习巩固了新学词汇，然后布置了作业。第二项作业遵循了学生好玩的天性，学习效果甚佳。

第三节　句型教学

案例1

牛津小学英语（苏教版）5B Unit 9 The English Club

Step 1　Warming up

T：Hello，boys and girls.

Ss：Hello，Miss Xu.

T：Nice to meet you.

Ss：Nice to meet you，too.

T：Ok. What's the date today?

S1：Today is 21st of October.

T：And what day is it today?

S2：It's Friday.

T：How about the weather?

S3：It's windy.

T：Yes. Sometimes it is cloudy and windy. And today we will learn Unit 9 The English Club.

T：Now Look at the screen，can you find my Chinese name?

S4：Your name is Yao Xiaoli.

T：Do you have an English name?

S4：My English name is Ellen.

T：Hello，Ellen. Can you find my English name?

（显示屏上出现“Shirley's list”）

T：This is my English name Shirley. Now look at Shirley's list. Do you want to know some information about Shirley? You may ask some questions.

S5：Where do you live?

T：I live in Century Garden. Where do you live?

S5：I live in Jiuhua Garden.

T：I hope one day I can visit you.

S6：Where are you from?

T：I am from Sanjiang Primary School. Are you from Sanjiang Primary School?

S6：Yes.

T：We are from the same school.

S7：How many people are there in your family? Who are they?

T：There are three people in my family. They are my husband，my daughter and I. You know husband?

Ss：丈夫。

T：Yes，he's my daughter's father. How many people are there in your family?

S7：There are three.

T：Yes，just like me. Right?

S7：Yes.

S8：What is your telephone number?

T：Look! This is my telephone number. It is 04517829. So if you have some problems with your homework，you can call me. And I think I can help you. I'm very glad to do that.

S9：What is your e-mail address?

T：My e-mail address is yxl403@163. com.

S10：what's your hobby?

T：Now look! I have some hobbies. I like travelling，watching cartoons and films with my daughter. Do you have any hobbies?

S10：My hobby is listening to music.

T：Do you like to watch cartoons and films?

Ss：Yes.

T：Maybe one day we can go to the cinema together.

Step 2　Presentation

T：Now look! This is a cartoon. Who is he?

S11：He is Monkey King.

T：When I was young，I like him very much. Read after me. Monkey King.

Ss：Monkey King.

T：Dou you know something about Monkey King? Here is a short passage about him. Please read the passage quickly and quietly and then try to answer the questions. 1. What does Monkey King like doing? 2. Where is he from?

Passage：

Sun Wukong is the king of monkey.

We call him Monkey King.

He is from China.

He is Chinese.

He speaks Chinese.

He likes helping others.

Learning tips：（学习小贴士）Extensive reading，catch the key sentences quickly.（泛读短文，迅速找出关键句。）

T：Ok. The first question. Who can?

S12：He likes helping others.

T：Do you like helping others?

S12：Yes.

T：Good girl.

T：And next，where is he from?

S13：He is from China.

T：Are you from China?

S13：Yes.

T：Of course. We are all from China. Do you love China?

S13：Yes.

T：Why?

S13：Because it is very large，and people in China are very friendly.

T：Good. Andy，why do you love China?

Andy：It is so beautiful and there are some interesting places in China.

T：I love China，too. Look，this is our motherland. You can see Yellow River. It is our mother river，you know.

T：Next，Yangtze River. Sometimes we call it Changjiang.

T：Last，the Great Wall，Tian'anmen，the Gardens of Suzhou，Bird's Nest and the Water Cube.

T：Our motherland is so beautiful and we love China more and more as time goes by because we are Chinese.

T：Can you describe Monkey King like this one?

Monkey king is from ________.（国家）

He is ________.（国籍）

He speaks ________.（语言）

S14：Where is Monkey King from?

S15：He is from China. He is Chinese. He speaks Chinese.

Step 3 Practice

T：Can you fill the blanks?

Star	Country	Nationality	Language
	China	China	Chinese
	the UK	Britain	English

续前表

Star	Country	Nationality	Language
	the USA	America	English
	Japan	Japan	Japanese

T：Let's do pair work.

S16：Where is Sun Wukong from?

S17：He is from China. He is Chinese. He speaks Chinese.

S16：Where is Harry Potter from?

S17：He is from the UK. He is British. He speaks English.

S16：Where is Minnie mouse from?

S17：She is from the USA. She is American. She speaks English.

S16：Where is Doraemon from?

S17：He is from Japan. He is Japanese. He speaks Japanese.

T：Excellent job. And I have a question for you. Are they from the same country?

Ss：No.

T：Of course they aren't. And I have two stars here. I can tell you they're from the same country. They are all from the UK. And they are Mascots of the Olympic Games. Their names are Wenlock.

T：They are very special. Look! This is a light. That means the taxi of London. And the special big eye means camera. It can take some photos. Can you find any rings? They mean the Olympic rings. So the main idea of the Olympic Game is "Quicker, higher and stronger". In Chinese, we say "更快、更高、更强". Do you want to visit London?

Ss：Yes!

T：Would you like to watch the Olympic Games?

Ss：Yes.

T：Of course we do. Now let's imagine：

1. Who will go to London in 2012?

2. Who will take part in the Olympic Games?

I can give you some advice：

I think ________ will go to London/take part in the Olympic Games.

Why?

Because…

Where is he/she from?

He/She is…

He/She speaks…

Pair work：

S18：I think Liu Xiang will go to London in 2012.

S19：Why?

S18：Because he is a famous runner.

S19：Where is he from?

S18：He is from China. He speaks Chinese.

S19：I think Obama will go to London in 2012.

S18：Why?

S19：Because he is the President of the United States.

S18：Where is he from?

S19：He is from the USA. He speaks English.

Step4 Production

T：I have a pen friend and I want to introduce her to you. Read the following passage and work in groups，discuss and find the answers.

My pen friend

Lily is my friend. She lives in America，but she is from the UK. She is Britain. Her father is from Japan and her mother is from the UK. They speak English.

She likes sport very much. At the weekends，she often goes climbing and plays table tennis with her friends. She's a good table tennis player. She wants to come to London because she likes watching Olympic Games.

Learning tips：Intensive reading，find the answer and underline it.

1. Lily lives in ________.

A. The UK　　B. the USA

2. Lily's mother is ________.

A. Chinese　　B. British

3. Lily likes ________.

A. sport　　B. reading

4. Can Lily play table tennis well? ________.

A. Yes, she can.　　B. No, she can't.

5. Why does she want to come to London? Because ________.

A. She can take part in Olympic Games.

B. She can watch Olympic Games.

Step 5 Summing up

Homework:

1. Write a short passage about your friends/teacher/family/favorite star…

2. Surf the internet, find some information about France and Australia.

案例1解析

这堂课的重点句型是：Where is he/she from? He/She is from… He/She speaks… He/She likes doing…

在准备环节，教师与学生一起谈论天气，相互交流，充分体现了人文关怀。

在呈现环节，教师先巧妙地运用"Shirley's list"复习了旧知识：Where do you live? I live in…接着教师询问学生：Where do you live? 跟着自然而然地说出I hope one day I can visit you. 这既复习了旧知识visit，又体现了人文关怀。在"Shirley's list"中还提供了一个telephone number信息，在回答完学生提问后，教师立即说出："If you have some problems with your homework, you can call me. And I think I can help you. I'm very glad to do that."这既体现了人文关怀，又复习了介词with。

接着教师通过学生喜爱的卡通人物孙悟空引入新课。我们知道，在句型教学中，教师应该设计各种情景让学生更好地理解句义。在这堂课中，教师共设计了四个情景：

第一个情景的设计是在呈现环节。教师通过引入卡通人物孙悟空导入新课，这极大地调动了学生的认知兴趣。接着教师通过让学生快速阅读一小段文章并回答问题，自然而然地呈现了新句型：He likes helping others. He is from China. 在此过程中，教师问学生："Are you from China? Do you love China? Why?"这三个问题很好地对学生进行了情感教育。教师还向同学们介绍了伟大祖国的名胜古迹，如黄河、长江、苏州园林、鸟巢、水立方等，进一步激发了学生的爱国热情。

第二个情景的设计是在操练环节。教师是利用图片来设计的，它给单调的句型教学增添了活力。教师设计了一张由四个明星组成的表格，他们是小学生非常熟悉和喜爱的孙悟空、哈利·波特、米妮和哆啦A梦。教师请学生填表说出这些人物各自的国家、国籍、语言等，这一情景的设计使学生进一步理解和掌握了新句型。

第三个情景的设计也是在操练环节，教师向学生介绍了两位来自同一个国家的明星——2012 年伦敦奥林匹克运动会吉祥物，然后请同学们想象一下谁会去伦敦，谁会参加奥运会。教师给大家建议，同学们思路大开，在特定的情景中自如地用新句型进行对话。

第四个情景的设计是在应用环节。教师先让大家读一篇短文，内容是为大家介绍一位笔友，然后让大家完成选择题。在此基础上，教师请同学们向大家介绍自己的朋友、家人或最喜爱的明星。这一情景的设计进一步巩固了新学的句型，强化了学生的交际能力。

在结课环节，教师布置了两个作业：1. Write a short passage about friends/teacher/family/favorite star…. 2. Surf the internet，find some information about France and Australia. 第一项作业有助于学生进一步巩固所学的新知识。第二项作业通过让学生找一找、查一查，克服了英语作业的封闭性。

案例 2

广州版《英语》（口语教材）B4 Unit 2 Success with English

Step 1　Warming up

T：These are some pictures of animals. Do you know what they are?

S1：They are rabbits.

S2：They are dogs.

S3：They are pigs.

Step 2　Presentation

T：Which animal do you like，Peter?

Peter：I like monkey.

T：You like monkeys. Oh，Peter likes monkeys. He likes monkeys.

（板书 Peter/He likes monkeys.）

T：Which one do you like，Rose?

Rose：I like sheep.

T：You like sheep. Oh，Rose likes sheep. She likes sheep.

（板书 Rose/She likes sheep.）

Step 3 Practice

T：I read English every day.（Alice）

S4：Alice reads English every day.

T：I go to work on foot.（Amanda）

S5：Amanda goes to work on foot.

T：Good. John，how does your father go to work?

John：He goes to work by car.

T：Yes，you got it.

Step 4 Production

T：I have magic. I know which animal you like. Do you believe me?

（教师做出神秘的表情，学生们都很好奇。）

只见教师走到Emily前面，很自信地说："You like rabbits，right?"

Emily：Yes!

教师翻开了合在Emily课桌上的卡片，卡片上真的是几只小兔。

Emily很惊讶，其他同学也很惊讶。老师怎么会知道的？同学们都来了兴致。

教师又来到Tony面前，很自信地说："Tony，you like lions. Right?"

Tony：Yes!

同学们发现老师好像真的有魔眼，于是争先恐后让老师猜猜自己的爱好。开始几个，老师都猜对了，但是接下来，老师开始犯错了，魔力似乎失效了。

T：Do you like elephants，Betty?

Betty：No，I…

T：No? Don't you like elephants?

Betty：No. I don't.

T：Oh，sorry. Do you like snakes?

Betty：No，I don't.

T：Oh，I lose the magic. I need help. Jane，what does Betty like?

Jane：She likes cats.

David：Maybe she likes geese?

同学们纷纷猜问，最后Betty翻开卡片，说："No，I don't. I like ducks."

T：Oh，she doesn't like geese. She likes ducks.

（板书 She doesn't like…She likes…）

T：Ask your partner，please! Try to know what he or she likes and what he or she doesn't like，then report.

S1：Linda likes bananas. She doesn't like oranges.

S2：Tom doesn't like kiwifruit，he likes cherries.

……

Step 5　Summing up

Today we learned I like… You like… We like… They like…

We also learned he likes… She likes… Mary likes… Tom likes…

Homework：

Ask your parents，please！ Try to know what your father or mother likes and what your father or mother doesn't like，write it down.

案例 2 解析

这堂课的重点句型是 Does he/she like…？No，he/she doesn't like…，He/She likes…。

在准备环节，教师通过询问同学们喜欢的动物这一极其生活化的问题一下子拉近了教师和学生的距离，也为新课做了自然的铺垫。

在呈现环节，教师依然问同学们喜欢的动物，但是在问完之后，教师加了一句 He/She likes…，渐渐地，学生们自己发现了一个规律：当句子中说明“谁”的这个词可以用 he 或 she 来代替时，句子中的动词要加 s。

在操练环节，教师通过变换人称的方式使学生进一步增强了对第三人称单数的分辨能力，使其准确地把握住了动词相应的变化，操练简单有效。

在应用环节，教师在让自己具有魔力和魔力丧失的过程中，引出了许多问句，这给了学生许多参与游戏、实践语言的机会，也加深了学生对目标语法点的理解。此外，询问伙伴的喜好这一真实语境的建立使同学们真正习得语言。

这堂课的结课环节进一步内化了学生的知识结构，使学生对所学的新知识形成完整的认知结构，布置的作业是对教学内容的拓宽和延伸。

第四节　对话教学

案例 1

牛津版《英语》（苏教版）5B Module 3 Unit 3 Changes

Step 1　Warming up

T：Good morning，class.

Ss：Good morning，teacher.

T：Let's listen and enjoy. Can you find the differences?

The cat is under the sofa. The table is next to the lamps. The picture is next to the window.

S1：The cat is on the sofa. The table is under the shelf. The picture is next to the shelf.

T：Very good.

Step 2　Presentation

T：Let's watch the flash and answer，who wants to move the furniture? Why?

(教师播放 flash)

Mum：Dad is coming next week. Let's give him a surprise!

Ben：OK，Mum. But what can we do?

Mum：Let's move the furniture!

Kitty：Sounds fun.

Mum：Let's put the sofa under the window first.

Ben：Great. And we can put the table next to the wall.

Kitty：Let's move the picture and lamps too.

Mum：Yes，let's do that.

(播放完毕)

S2：Mum wants to move the furniture because she wants to give Dad a surprise.

T：Yes. Let's learn "surprise". Give him a surprise.

Now，let's choose and say，

I'm…

My dad is…

We want to…

So we…

S3：I'm Eric.

My Dad is coming this Friday.

We want to give him a surprise.

So we move the furniture.

T：Amazing. What furniture do they want to move? Watch the flash again and answer.

S4：They want to put the sofa under the window first. And then put the table next to the wall. Finally，they want to move the picture and lamps too.

T：Great!

Step 3　Practice

T：Look at the pictures and talk about the furniture. Try to say,

We want to move…

It is…

Let's put it…

S5：We want to move the clock.

It is on the wall.

Let's put it on the shelf.

Step 4　Production

T：Now work in pairs. Talk about the moving list and try to introduce the differences.

Moving list：

mirror

teddy bear

football

table

sofa

……

S6：My Dad is coming the day after tomorrow. I want to give him a surprise!

S7：Really? What can you do?

S6：I can move the furniture!

S7：Sounds fun.

S6：I want to put the football on the TV first. And I can put the table next to the piano.

S7：You're so great!

T：Look at the screen. This is Kitty's bedroom. You please help Kitty move the furniture and introduce.

S6：Let's move the furniture to give Kitty a surprise.

S7：What can we do?

S6：Let's put the toy beetle under the bed.

S7：It's a good idea.

S6：What about moving the sofa?

S7：Can we put it next to the computer desk?

S6：Sounds great.

S7：Let's do that.

Step 5　Summing up

Homework:

1. Copy the new words.
2. Read the text.
3. Plan to move the furniture in your bedroom and introduce it.

案例 1 解析

这堂课是典型的对话教学课。

在准备环节，教师通过找不同激发学生的学习兴趣，并引出课题：furniture。

在呈现环节，教师主要是让学生听懂 Mum，Kitty 和 Ben 之间的文本对话，使学生了解了他们搬家具的原因，并从中提取出所搬动家具的相关信息。这种整体呈现对话文本的方式是我们提倡的。接着教师再一次让学生听对话文本，并用问题进行检测，从而引出新授内容，并重点操练：We plan to move the…，Let's put the….

在这堂课的操练环节教师设计了看图片编对话的活动。因为感知和理解不能代替运用，所以操练需要不同的层次和阶段，看图片编对话属于意义操练，对话的创编可以更好地让学生运用目标知识，它比机械操练更具真实性、趣味性和实用性。

在应用环节教师请同学们帮助 Kitty 制定卧室搬家具计划，从实际出发，提高了学生的语言能力。由此可见，对话的拓展训练是对话教学的重要组成部分，它是对对话知识运用的一种反映，是对话知识运用的提炼和升华。既为对话，就应以听懂、会说为主。如果对话教学就是直接读句子或写句子，那么学生就失去了思维、理解、体验的过程。

在节课环节，这堂课的作业布置新颖、有趣，它既可以激发学生的学习兴趣，又能发展学生的语言能力，这种与学生日常生活密切联系的作业不仅达到了让学生复习所学知识的目的，还激发了学生的潜能，从而能更好地促进学生接受新知识和进行创造性学习。

案例 2

《英语》(PEP 版) 五年级下册 Unit 4

Step 1　Warming up

T: Good morning, everyone. Let's sing "What Are You Doing" together, Ok?

Ss: Ok!

T: Wonderful. Now I will show you some pictures. Can you tell me in English?

S1：She is reading a book.

T：Very nice. Let's go on.

S2：She is drawing pictures.

T：Well-done. Try again.

S3：Mum is cooking dinner.

T：You're great! The last picture.

S4：She is answering the mobile phone.

T：You are acute. Now let's have a guessing game.

Step 2 Presentation

（让一名学生抽取一张卡片，然后躲在讲台后面，教师带领其他同学问："What are you doing?" 抽取卡片的学生站起来边做相应的动作边回答。请 5～6 名学生轮流上来抽卡片，直到全班同学初步会说句型 "What are you doing?"）

T：Listen to the tape and answer the questions：

（1）What is Mike doing?

（2）What is Alice doing?

S5：Mike is washing the clothes.

S6：Alice is playing the piano.

T：Good. Let's do pair work.

（学生2人一组，分角色练习对话。学生拿出事先准备好的图片、玩具或实物，两两进行对话操练。）

Step 3 Practice

T：Activity 1，listen and tick.

Activity 2，sentence relay.

（每一组从第一位同学开始，用"Hello，what are you doing?"提问，第二位同学回答后转身问第三位同学。要使每位同学都有操练的机会，同学发现错误可当场指出。）

Activity 3，making telephone calls.

（学生2人一组，每人在一张纸条上面写一个动词短语的ing形式，如emptying the trash，然后两人交换纸条，分别将纸条卷起来作道具，根据各自手中纸条的内容模拟打电话。）

Activity 4，let's play.

（请1名学生上来，背对其他同学站好，台下任意一位同学问："What are you doing?"站在前面的同学边做动作边回答。其他同学根据听到的回答在表格里做好记录。然后换一名同学上来，接着做游戏。）

Step 4 Production

Story time：

Lucy：Hello，Alice. What are you doing?

Alice：I'm watching TV. What about you?

Lucy：I'm doing my homework. What are your parents doing?

Alice：My father is reading newspaper and my mother is cooking dinner.

Lucy：Is your sister reading a book?

Alice：No，she isn't. She's drawing pictures.

T：What are Alice's parents doing? Is Alice's sister playing games?

Step 5　Summing up

T：What do we learn today?

（板书 What are you doing? I am…）

Homework：

Finish exercises on your activity manual.

案例 2 解析

对话教学一直是小学英语教学中的难点。这堂课围绕“What Are You Doing?”这个核心话题来展开对话教学，它不仅贴近学生的生活实际，而且富有很强的实用性和趣味性。

在准备阶段，师生共唱“What are you doing”，既复习了有关的动词词组，又最大限度地激活了学生学习英语的兴趣。接着教师组织学生看图说话，既复习了旧知识，又培养了学生用英语思维的能力。

在呈现环节，教师通过游戏来导入新课，使学生的兴致提高，课堂气氛相当活跃。接着教师又创设新的情景让学生参与其中。在理解之后，教师让学生拿出事先准备好的道具开展 pair work，使学生又活跃了起来。

在操练环节，教师共设计了 4 项活动。活动 1 主要是培养学生听的能力，活动 2 既练习了语言，又培养了合作精神，活动 3 使对话充满了乐趣，活动 4 让学生在游戏中自然而然地巩固了新知识。

在应用环节，教师通过一则对话小故事训练学生的听和说，其实还可以试着让学生演一演。

本堂课的结课环节虽然简单，但是板书的形式值得推荐，板书对教学内容进行了很好的概括，使这堂课的脉络清晰、有条理。

第五节　语篇教学

案例 1

《新标准英语》4B Unit 2 London is the Capital of England

Step 1　Warming up

T：Hi，boys and girls.

Ss：Hi，Jessica.

T：Let's sing a song：London Bridge is Falling Down.

Step 2　Presentation

T：Where is London Bridge?

S1：It's in London.

T：Where is London?

S2：It's in England.

T：Good. Now let's talk about London.

S3：London is the capital of the UK.

S4：It's beautiful.

S5：It has the famous river —Thames.

S6：Big Ben is very big and old.

T：You are so great.

T：Let's watch the flash.

Look，this is the River Thames.

It's long and wide.

This is the Big Ben.

It's very tall and old.

This is Tower Bridge.

It's very famous.

This is Hyde Park.

It's very beautiful.

Step 3　Practice

T：London is the capital of the UK. Which city is the capital of China?

Ss：Beijing.

T：Now let's talk about Beijing.

S7：Beijing is big and beautiful.

S8：The Great Wall is in Beijing.

S9：Tian'anmen Square is in Beijing.

T：There are many other famous places in Beijing. Look and Guess.

Forbidden City

Summer Palace

National Grand Theatre

It has a history of over 600 years. It was the home of emperors and their families.

(Forbidden City)

It is an old and beautiful garden. It has three hills and Kunming Lake.

(Summer Palace)

It is the modern attraction of Beijing. It is a short walk away from Tian'anmen Square and the south gate of Forbidden City.

(National Grand Theatre)

Step 4　Production

Group Work：A Survey

Describe other countries' capitals.

G1：Cairo is the capital of Egypt. It has the famous site—Pyramids. It is one of the Seven Wonders of the World. It also has the Great Sphinx. It is a carving. It has lion's body and king's head. It symbolizes strength and wisdom. Cairo is a cradle of civilization. Food in Cairo is hot and spicy. A journey through Cairo is a journey through time.

G2：Washington D. C. is the capital of the United States of America. The city is named after George Washington—the first president of United States. "The President's House" is called the White House. It has many museums and monuments. The flower is the American Beauty Rose.

G3：Moscow is the capital of Russia. The city is named after the river—Moskva River. People there like to eat caviar. They love mushrooms very much. Red Square is the landmark building in Moscow. Kremlin is the symbol of Russia government.

G4：Tokyo is the capital of Japan. It is one of the biggest and most crowded cities. It is filled with factories，large office buildings，banks，restaurants and shops of all sizes. Many people move from other parts of Japan to attend college and then work in Tokyo. The cherry blossom season is in late March and early April. It's very popular.

Step 5 Summing up

Homework：

(1) 学生将了解到的有关各国首都的情况，用英语向父母和同学讲一讲。

(2) 模仿跟读课文录音带。

(3) 抄写文中的重点句。

案例1解析

这堂课成功利用了教材这个载体，努力挖掘教材的潜力，是语篇教学的一个很好的尝试。通过语篇，学生吸收语言点，了解国内外文化知识，拓展语言，进而进行实际交流。语篇教学的最终目的是提高学生综合运用英语的能力。

在准备环节，教师通过一首歌曲充分调动学生的热情，将学生的目光一下子集中到了英国的风景名胜上。这一情景的设计是有意义的，为学生创造了产生语篇的条件。

在呈现环节，教师通过问答的形式自然而然地为学生创设了有效的语言环境，使学生在真实的交际环境中习得语言、运用语言。这种从整体开始、进入部分、再回到整体的方式是值得提倡的。

在操练环节，教师通过谈谈在首都北京的活动自然过渡，在过程中渗透文化，学生做到了操练词不离句，从文本信息和插图获取相关元素，在整体情境中运用语言。

在应用环节，教师让学生分成四组开展调查并做展示，这极大地激发了学生学习英语的兴趣，培养了学生的语言应用能力，让学生学了会说，有了成功的体验，还拓展了文化知识。这种紧扣文本、围绕主题进行拓展的方式是有效的语言输出的保障。

在结课环节，这堂课的作业有基础的，也有灵活的。这种分层次的作业有利于培养学生的创造性思维。

案例 2

《新世纪小学英语》3B Unit 8 Enjoy Reading

Step 1　Warming up

T：Hello，boys and girls. Are you ready? Let's enjoy a song "My Happy School".

My happy school is lots of fun.

My happy school is fun.

I learn with everyone.

Come play with everyone.

……

Step 2　Presentation

T：Thank you. Our school is fun. What do you do at school?

Grace：I read books at school.

Tony：I play basketball with my friends.

John：I learn much knowledge at school.

T：Grace says she likes reading at school. Do you like reading?

Ss：Yes!

T：What do you like reading? Why?

S1：I like reading story books because they are interesting.

S2：I like reading music books because they tell me how to sing.

S3：I like reading picture books because they are fun.

T：Good. Some books tell us stories. These are story books.

Some books show us many pictures.

Ss：Those are picture books.

T：Some books show us how to play and sing music.

Ss：They are music books.

T：Children like reading art-and-craft books and science books. Many people like reading magazines and newspapers. They are our good friends.

T：Today I got a book for you. It's from Anthony Browne. He is from the UK. Let's have a look at the book.

My Mum

The name of his book is ________________.

It is a ____________________.

T: What's the name of this book?

What kind of the book is?

S4: The name of this book is My Mum. It's a picture book.

T: Good. Let's find out the main idea. What does the book tell us? Please read this picture book. (silent reading)

It tells us ____________________.

S5: It tells us mum is a super mum.

S6: It tells us mum is very nice.

S7: It tells us mum is a fantastic cook.

T: Very good. Try to get details from the book.

S8: She's nice, my mum. My mum is a fantastic cook. She can cook dinner for me.

T: Amazing. Read after me. Fantastic, fantastic.

T: Is your mum a fantastic cook?

S9: My mum is a fantastic cook. She can cook meat for me.

S10: My mum is a fantastic cook. She can cook fish for me.

S11: My mum is a fantastic cook. She can cook dumplings for me.

……

T: Are they Yummy?

Ss: Yes!

T: So mum can cook. She can paint, too. She is a magic painter. She can paint herself and the wall of the house.

T: Mum is painting herself. That means mum is making herself more beautiful. She can paint the wall of the house.

S12：My mum is a magic painter. She can paint the wall.

S13：My mum is a magic painter. She can paint the chair.

S14：My mum is a magic painter. She can paint the table.

T：Now we know two details of “my mum”. One is “my mum” is a fantastic cook. The other is “my mum” is a magic painter. Do you want to know more about mum?

Ss：Yes!

T：Listen carefully.

She’s very nice.

My mum is a great gardener.

She can make anything grow.

T：Can you find gardener in the word bank?

Ss：No.

T：Sometimes we can guess the meaning of the word. For example，farm，farmer. The farmer works in the farm. So gardener works in the ________.

Ss：Garden.

T：Follow me，gardener. Let’s see how great mum is?

（视频演示妈妈种花的过程）

S15：Mum can make flowers grow.

T：Mum can make anything grow.

T：Look at the picture. What is Mum? My mum is a big boss. She can make anything come true. Follow me，boss. Now let’s enjoy some pictures.

T：The baby wants some toy trucks. Mum can buy the toy truck for him.

S15：Children want to swim. Mum can take them to the swimming pool.

S16：The boy wants to be tall. He can sit on mum's back.

S17：Children want to read books. Mum can read a book with babies.

T：Mum can make our dreams come true. There are two details in this passage. Can you find them?

Ss：Mum is a big boss. Mum is a great gardener.

T：She's really，really nice，my mum. My mum is a good fairy. She is beautiful like a butterfly.

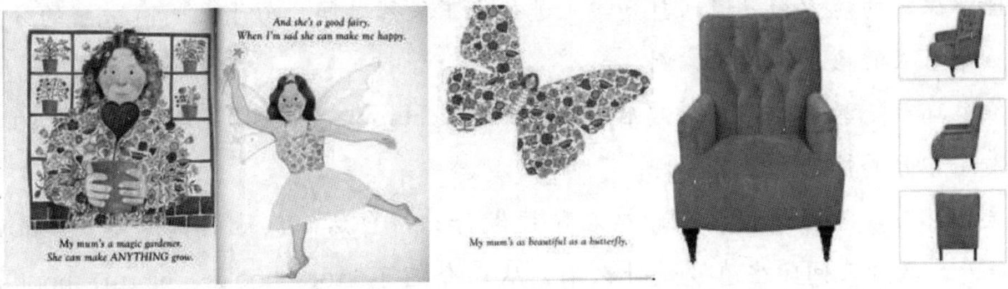

She is comfortable like an armchair. You know sitting in the armchair is comfortable. Follow me，comfortable. Tell me how is your mum? Is your mum a good fairy?

S18：My mum is beautiful like a princess.

T：Is your father handsome like a prince?

S18：Yes!

Step 3　Practice

T：Who can say five details together?

S19：My mum is a fantastic cook. My mum is a magic painter. My mum is a great gardener. My mum is a big boss. My mum is a good fairy.

T：Big hands. Do you love your mum? Let's read it beautifully.

T：Fantastic. Do you like reading the book?

Ss：Yes.

T：And how do you think of the book?

I think this book is ________________.

I enjoy reading it.

S20：I think this book is wonderful. I enjoy reading it.

S21：I think this book is vivid. I enjoy reading it.

……

Step 4　Production

T：Prepare for the reading report.

Step 5 Summing up

Homework:

(1) Have a look at the book.

(2) Find out the main idea.

(3) Audio homework.

案例 2 解析

这堂课将语音、词汇和语法巧妙而真实地融为一体，对课文进行整体教学，培养学生从整体理解课文的能力和习惯，引导学生进行上下段落之间、句子之间有联系的分析和学习，是一个有效的语篇教学的案例。

在准备环节，教师和学生一起欣赏并唱“My Happy School”，调动了学生的学习热情，激发了学习的情感，效果很好。

在呈现环节，教师通过询问学生在学校做什么，自然而然地引出课题“Enjoy reading”，接着，教师又问学生喜欢读什么书，从而介绍了 story books，picture books，music books，art-and-craft books，science books，magazines，newspapers。最后，教师拿出一本书，向大家介绍了书名和作者，问大家它属于哪一类书，同学们异口同声地回答“picture book”。这一烘托背景的方法值得推荐，因为背景知识的缺乏会造成理解的困难。在语篇阅读教学中，教师紧紧围绕五个细节精心设计问题，并通过这些贯穿语篇主线的问题，指导学生了解语篇内容，引导学生在阅读过程中抓住主要信息，进而培养学生的信息加工能力和阅读能力。这堂课语篇教学分析的重点在三个方面：一是熟悉每个语段的重要语句，掌握语段所提供的信息；二是分析文章遣词造句的特点，包括语句之间、上下语段之间的衔接和呼应，连句成篇的语法手段；三是引导学生归纳文章的主题，了解作者的写作意图。教师通过对话、小组讨论、多媒体展示等手段，成功地使学生读懂了文章，并通过回答问题提高了语言表达能力。

在操练环节，教师让学生脱口说出语篇的五个细节，这对学生的表达能力是一个挑战，同时也增强了学生的自信心。在这一环节，教师还指导学生有感情地朗读课文，要读出对妈妈的爱。这一做法能逐步培养学生的语感，让学生在朗读中夯实基础，提高能力。

在应用环节，教师让学生以小组为单位做阅读报告，这样能使学生综合地运用所学的语言知识把单项的语言技能转变为运用语言交换信息的能力。

在结课环节，教师布置了三项作业。第一、第二项作业能培养学生的观察、记忆、思维等多种能力，第三项作业为有声作业，就是让学生把这一课的内容复述出来并录为语音，由教师进行检查打分的一种口语作业形式，这种作业重视语言的运用，能让学生感受作业带来的成功与喜悦。

图书在版编目（CIP）数据

小学英语教学设计与案例解析 / 王融，董玲主编
. --2 版 . --北京：中国人民大学出版社，2024.1
21 世纪小学教师教育系列教材 / 惠中总主编
ISBN 978-7-300-32066-3

Ⅰ.①小… Ⅱ.①王… ②董… Ⅲ.①英语课一教学设计一小学一师资培养一教材 Ⅳ.①G623.312

中国国家版本馆 CIP 数据核字（2023）第 148095 号

21 世纪小学教师教育系列教材
总主编 惠 中
小学英语教学设计与案例解析（第二版）
主编 王融 董玲
Xiaoxue Yingyu Jiaoxue Sheji yu Anli Jiexi

出版发行 中国人民大学出版社			
社 址 北京中关村大街 31 号		**邮政编码** 100080	
电 话 010 - 62511242（总编室）		010 - 62511770（质管部）	
010 - 82501766（邮购部）		010 - 62514148（门市部）	
010 - 62515195（发行公司）		010 - 62515275（盗版举报）	
网 址 http://www.crup.com.cn			
经 销 新华书店			
印 刷 天津鑫丰华印务有限公司		**版 次** 2019 年 7 月第 1 版	
开 本 787 mm×1092 mm 1/16		2024 年 1 月第 2 版	
印 张 12		**印 次** 2024 年 1 月第 2 次印刷	
字 数 239 000		**定 价** 36.00 元	

版权所有 侵权必究 印装差错 负责调换

教学支持说明

（教学课件）

中国人民大学出版社教育学科秉承“出教材学术精品，育人文社科英才”的出版宗旨，多年来，出版了大批高质量的教育学、小学教育、学前教育专业教材和学术著作。

我们为本教材制作了相应的 PPT 教学课件，任何一位采用本书作为授课教材的教师均可免费获得该课件。为了确保该课件仅为授课教师获得，烦请您填写如下材料，并将相关信息通过 E-mail 发送给我们，我们将在收到相关信息后通过 E-mail 给您发送该课件。欢迎您加入我们的 QQ 群（教育新视野交流群，群号为 159813080），或登录我社官方网站（www. crup. com. cn），注册并认证成为教师会员，以获得更好的服务。

我们的联系方式：

地址：（100872）北京市中关村大街甲 59 号文化大厦 1202 室

中国人民大学出版社

电话：（010）62515955　62515383

E-mail：ggglcbfs@vip. 163. com

QQ 群：159813080

兹证明__________大学/学院__________院/系__________专业__________学年第__________学期开设的__________课程，采用中国人民大学出版社出版的__________（书名、作者）作为本课程教材。授课教师为__________，授课班级共________个、学生________人。授课教师需要与本书配套的教学课件。

联 系 人：____________________

通信地址：____________________

邮　　编：____________________

电　　话：____________________

E-mail：____________________

系/院主任：__________（签字）

（系/院办公室章）

________年______月______日